Famines and Famine Relief - An Andhra Zamindari in 19th Century

Famines and Famine Relief -
An Andhra Zamindari in 19th Century

K.S.S. Seshan

GYAN

Published, 2020

Published by

Gyan Publishing House
5, Ansari Road
Daryaganj, New Delhi-110002
Phone: 011-47034999, 9811692060
www.gyanbooks.com
E-mail: books@gyanbooks.com

Printed at: Gyan Press, Delhi.

Cataloging in Publication Data—DK
Courtesy: D.K. Agencies (P) Ltd. <docinfo@dkagencies.com>

Seshan, K. S. S., 1941- **author.**
Famines and famine relief : an Andhra zamindari in 19th century / Prof. K.S.S. Seshan.
pages cm
Includes bibliographical references.
ISBN 9788121219945

1. Famines—India—Punganuru—History—19th century. 2. Food relief—India—Punganuru—History—19th century. 3. Land tenure—India—Punganuru—History—19th century. 4. Agricultural systems—India—Punganuru—History—19th century. I. Title.

LCC HC438.P86S47 2020 | DDC 363.883095485 23

Contents

Foreword

My gracious friend Professor K.S.S. Seshan has honoured me by asking me to write a foreword to his detailed study of the agrarian history of a subdistrict in what is now the Chittoor district of Andhra, for a period of one hundred years (the nineteenth century). This sub-district had its headquarters at Punganur or Punganuru (13°23'N., 78°34'E.), a place close to where the borders of Andhra meet those of Tamilnadu in the south and Karnataka in the west. It was seized from Mysore by the English in 1799 and annexed to the Madras Presidency, which soon thereafter expanded with the annexation of the Carnatic and of the Ceded districts received from Hyderabad. The Madras Presidency came to be known within the next three decades for its Ryotwari system; but Panganur became an exception. It was, like Bengal and the Northern Circars of the Madras Presidency, kept under a Permanent Settlement made with its raja or chief.

This fact alone justifies a special study of the Panganur 'zamīndārī', which Professor K.S.S. Seshan has now carried out with a most creditable exploration of all the relevant archives. He first traces for us the revenue and administrative arrangements of the territory, with the zamīndārī being obliged to pay a large fixed amount annually designated as *peshkash* (tribute) to the British government, while he dealt with the peasantry through his own establishment.

Professor Seshan then leads us to his main theme, the famines in the area, especially the famine of 1876-78. According to R.C. Dutt; five million people perished in the Madras Presidency in a single year of this famine.

General histories, like V.A. Smith's *Oxford History of India*, tell us that the Madras Government gravely mismanaged the situation, once the famine broke out. The then Viceroy Lord Lytton was generous with his censure. Part of the reason for this was the Madras Government's total famine expenditure viz. £ 10 million (Rs 150 crore), compared to the Bombay Government's expenditure of just £ 4 million (Rs 60 crore). Professor Seshan describes for us the limited nature of relief provided by the British government, and then, on the insistence of officials from Calcutta, like R.C. Temple, lowering the wages paid on public works, precisely when the prices were rocketing. The inhumanity of it all still sickens one.

We should all be grateful to Professor Seshan for the detailed study of the economy and administration of a locality during the 19th century that he offers us. It brings to life the past of a locality that really needed a biographer like him.

— **Irfan Habib**
Professor Emeritus,
Aligarh Muslim University, Aligarh

Preface

"Our Sweetest songs are those
that tell of Saddest Thought" – **P.B. Shelley**

Famines in India, under the British rule, do bring us such saddest thought. The present study "Famines and Famine Relief - An Andhra Zamindari in 19th Century" deals with the incidence of Famines and the Famine relief measures in Punganur Zamindari during the 19th. Century and tries to assess the kind of relief measures provided to alleviate the suffering of the people. This study is an off-shoot of my earlier work on the British relations with Punganur Zamindari, which was published as British Role in Rural Economy (New Delhi, 1989). The frequent references to the acute famines in the Zamindari during the rule of the British that I came across while researching, drew me on to a more detailed study of the impact of the famines in Punganur Zamindari under the dual rule of the Zamindar and the British government. The period chosen is the 19th century when British colonialism reached its heyday even in its relations with the Zamindars.

The present study hence seeks to analyze at a micro level the economic profile of Punganur under the indirect rule of the British, the occurrence of Famines and scarcities, as well as the consequent measures adopted by 1. The Zamindar and 2. The Government. The study is specifically limited to one particular Zamindari, Punganur in the erstwhile Madras

Presidency, now in Chittoor District of Andhra Pradesh. Though Punganur was a compact administrative unit under the authority of the Zamindar, the British government had under its control every other power except the revenue collections that was entrusted to the Zamindar.

Punganur Zamindari presents certain unique features. Firstly it was the only Palem in the Ceded Districts, now familiarly known as Rayalaseema, which was not dispossessed by the British though such Palems were all sequestrated by Thomas Munro when he was the Principal Collector during 1800-1807. Secondly, in the case of other Zamindars in the Madras Presidency, either permanent Sanads were issued or completely dispossessed, in the case of Punganur, the Zamindar was kept under temporary leases from 1799, when parts of it were brought under the British control, and a permanent Sanad was issued only in 1861. Thirdly, this Zamindari unlike others passed through several systems of land tenures like Ryotwari (introduced by Munro himself), Kulwari (Village Settlement), and finally Zamindari. Yet another uniqueness in this Zamindari was the prevalence of numerous revenue settlements during the 19th century like the Annual, Triennial, Quinquennial, Decennial, and finally the Permanent Settlement. The study presupposes that the concept of *Indirect Rule* was in operation in the Zamindari as far as matters like Famine relief were concerned.

The study has as its frame of reference the following factors relating to Famines in Punganur during the 19th century:

1. Land Tenural structures prevalent under the colonial set up in the Zamindari.
2. The types of revenue settlements to which the Zamindari was subjected to by the Government.
3. Agricultural practices and cropping patterns in Punganur during the study period.

4. The major famines and scarcities in the Zamindari and the sufferings of the ryots.
5. The relief measures the Zamindar took to provide relief to the people during such scarcities.
6. The steps the Government initiated to ameliorate the sufferings of the people besides providing relief to the Zamindar whose responsibility was to collect the land rents and administer the Zamindari.

For the purpose of the present study a number of primary sources have been consulted. With the systematic destruction of records by the Zamindars themselves at the time of the abolition of the Zamindari, a good number of records are lost to the researcher and it is not an easy task to locate and trail in to have access to the surviving records available at unexpected and discreet places. In as much as the Zamindari records are obviously linked to land disputes and consequent court cases, a lot of persuasion besides perseverance was needed to establish rapport with the holders of such records to have access to them. It is only when the academic nature of the study is established and the lurking phobia removed, one can gain access to the hitherto unexplored valuable records preserved in the houses of the relatives and former officials of the successive Zamindars.

Zamindari records in many ways are different from the records maintained by the government now mostly preserved in the Archives like the National Archives, New Delhi, A.P. State Archives, Tarnaka, Hyderabad, and the Regional Office of State Archives, Tirupati.(ROSAT), which were also consulted for the present study. The Departmental Reports of the Government, the proceedings of the Board of Revenue, the District Records, the Retained Disposals, the Fortnightly Reports, the Collectors' correspondence with the successive Zamindars, Reports of the Divisional Officers on the Zamindari have been of great use for the study. But as the present study being limited to a small unit of administration not more than few Mandals of the present set up, perusal of micro level records pertaining to this region was imperative.

The distinct Zamindari records like the *Goshwara* Accounts, *Jamabandy* Accounts, Day Books, Manuals of Rules, Letters, Petitions and Arzis, Memorials of the Zamindars, Sale Deeds, Court Judgments, Sanads, *Kabuliyats* (statements of acceptance) and numerous other documents that evade any specific categorization have been extensively consulted after locating them. In addition to the remnants of the Zamindari records preserved at various places, sometimes within the family circle of the Zamindars and elsewhere, records at District Collectorates in Chittoor, Cuddapah and Vellore; Taluk Katcheries, Panchayat Samithis and at the Village officers, were made use of. Personal collections of few distant relatives of the erstwhile Zamindars and the Judicial papers with the families of lawyers at Chittoor who dealt with the Zamindars' court cases earlier were of immense use for the present study.

While attempting to study the famine situations and the deprivation of the people at the Zamindari level, the study also tries to analyze the economic topography of the Zamindari, taking into consideration the interlinked rural economic factors like land tenural structures, the periodical revenue settlements, the general agricultural practices, crops, cropping pattern, irrigational facilities etc. as these are generally the indicators of the prosperity or otherwise of the peasantry. They are in more than one way, the economic parameters of a given area. These factors also reflect the extent to which the peasants can withstand from adverse situations arising out of failure of monsoons. Famines were not only the result of lack of rains and droughts but also because of the absence of governmental initiatives, unfavorable land tenures, unfair methods of taxation and a host of other factors. Therefore this study addresses itself to have an understanding of the economic situation by analyzing the basic rural economic factors in the Zamindari during the 19th century.

This study is divided into nine chapters and the first four are devoted to provide historical background of the Zamindari, the land tenural structures and land revenue settlements and the agricultural practices respectively. The fifth and sixth chapters deal with famines in Punganur during the early phase 1800-1860, and 1860-1870. The impact of the Great Famine of 1876-78 is exclusively dealt as the seventh chapter. The 1891-92 famine, considered to be also very widespread, is discussed in the eighth chapter. The last chapter is about the major findings of the study.

Several significant primary documents which have a bearing on the study, like the letters of Hyder Ali of Mysore, Lord Cornwallis, the Governor –General, Sir Charles Wood, the Secretary of State for India, and others are appended at the end of the volume. The entire text of the Sanad that ensured the Permanent Settlement of the Punganur Zamindari, granted in 1861, after several repeated urges on the part of the Zamindar, is also given as an Appendix. The famines and the methods adopted by the Zamindar and the government in extending relief in Punganur, provide a microcosm of what happened at the larger Presidency level.

K.S.S. Seshan

Acknowledgements

The present volume was made possible through a study carried under the University Grants Commission (UGC) funded project, *Famines and Famine Relief Measures in Punganur Zamindari: 1800-1948*, for which an extensive field study was conducted. The preliminary study of the primary sources revealed that a large number of vital documents on the subject were available at the India office Library, (now part of British Library) London. A visit to the United Kingdom to collect source materials was made possible by the award of a Visitorship of the British Council. The travel to the U.K. was sponsored by the Indian Council for Historical Research (ICHR). I therefore thank the UGC, the British Council and the ICHR, for their grants. Besides, the travel grants enabled me to visit few Universities like Oxford, Swansea and Manchester where I could meet experts in the field like Barbara Harris - White, Marica Clark, Jocelyn Kynch, Michael Moguruby, Windy Wolsen and others. I thank them as I was immensely benefited at the thoughtful insights they provided on the subject of my study.

I express my sincere gratitude to Professor Irfan Habib, the doyen among the contemporary historians in the country for bestowing great interest in my present study, and affectionately obliging me to write a foreword for the book.

I was greatly benefited by the numerous discussions I had with Prof. D.N. Reddy, former Dean, School of Social Sciences, University of Hyderabad, who read my earlier drafts and made valuable suggestions at every stage of this study. I thank him profusely for all the help he rendered.

I gratefully acknowledge the unstinted cooperation and help extended by the late, Sugutoor (Aminigunta) Sankar Royal, a scion of the Punganur Zamindar's family for allowing me to have access to the large pile of private papers in his possession (credited as A.S.R. Collections in this study). I also thank Sugutoor Rajendra, a member of the Punganur Zamindari family, now a Senior Advocate of the Madanapalle Bar, for all the help he extended, and whose enduring friendship I always cherished.

I also thank Kulvanth Aurora, the London based art critic, whose enlightened company was a stimulus for finding answers to his searching and thought provoking queries on my study.

I thank the Directors and their very helpful staff at the State Archives, Tarnaka, Hyderabad, the Tamil Nadu State Archives, Egmore, Chennai and the Archivist at Regional Office of the State Archives at Tirupati. (ROSAT) for extending me all the help. My thanks are due to Prof. G.N. Rao of the Centre For Development Studies, (CDS) Trivandrum, Prof. S.A.R. Sastry of Andhra University and Prof. R. Radhakrishna, former Dean at the University of Hyderabad for their keen interest in my study and for offering very valuable suggestions. To Prof. S. Viswanathan, former Dean of Humanities at the University of Hyderabad, I owe my thanks for making very helpful suggestions. I express my thanks to Prof. Ishrat Alam, Chairman and Co-ordinator, Centre for Advanced Studies, Department of History, AMU for all the help he rendered.

I thank my daughter Ms. Shatpada for her meticulous scrutiny of all the chapters and providing valuable insights besides painstakingly proofreading. I thank Mr. M.C.V. Prasad, Mr. Yashwanth Sugutoor and Ms. M.C. Vennela for all the trouble they have taken in copy editing the manuscript.

I thank Mr. Amit Garg and his able staff at Messrs. Gyan Publishers, New Delhi, for bringing out the book so well and in such a short period.

K.S.S. Seshan

I

Introduction

Though Famines were not unknown to India prior to colonial rule, they were few and far between. They were also highly localized and only the areas hit by natural calamities like drought were affected. But under the British, famines in India were more severe, more frequent and more widespread. While in the 17th and 18th. Centuries, famines and scarcities were mostly due to failure of monsoons and political disturbances, the 19th. Century, when British rule in India got entrenched, in contrast, witnessed as many as twelve major Famines in South India alone besides numerous scarcities. It is not only the failure of crops, migration of people due to scarcities, large scale deaths due to starvation, incendiarism, sale of children by the very parents in order to save their lives, but also the death of cattle for want of water and fodder etc., were all the distinguishing features of the 19th. Century famines in India.

The word 'Famine', derived from the Latin word '*fames*' meaning hunger, is defined as a condition of extreme general scarcity of food or want of food, hunger and starvation in a certain area or part of a country.[1] It may therefore connote broadly as a widespread shortage of food, caused by natural calamities or shortfall of rain or due to swarms of insects and pests, leading to distress and starvation of people over a large area. It may be the result of drought due to lack of rains or on account of scarcity that results due to insufficiency of food supply. Droughts and scarcities are generally confined comparatively to limited localities and last but for short periods of time. Famines sometimes may be caused only by human factors as in the case of Bengal Famine of 1943. They might be the result of historical and economic factors such as war, trade depressions, or even heavy land taxes. Any study on famines therefore involves an inquiry not only into local and contemporary climatic and agricultural conditions, but also that of political, economic and social conditions in the broadest sense.

Famines in India, as L.C.A. Knowles aptly pointed out, "is a lockout in the agricultural industry."[2] As agriculture has been the main occupation of the majority of the people in the country, such lockouts did affect the entire country. Agriculture not only supplied food grains and raw materials like cotton, jute and oil seeds, but it also provided occupation to about seventy five percent of population directly or indirectly.

To ensure normal cropping, it is important that the seasonal distribution of rainfall is normal, occur at the right time and be well distributed. When this did not happen, generally famines have occurred. General economic conditions of the country also have a close bearing on famines. If the masses are economically strong, few failures of crops would not affect much, but if they have no savings to fall back upon, even a slight drought would cause a severe suffering to them. The severity of famines in India during the nineteenth century was largely due to deterioration in the economic condition of the people.[3] The victims of these famines were counted in millions. There is also a fair amount of agreement among nineteenth century economic historians and commentators regarding the causes for these catastrophes. In most cases, famines were due to massive crop failure on account of droughts. The immediate impact of these crop failures was not only to reduce the food availability, but more importantly to shatter the rural economy. Landless agricultural laborers in particular found little employment as agricultural activity was brought to a standstill. Food prices increased, and hoarding became common. Trade was often slow and food grains generally were not promptly moved from places of plenty to places of scarcity. The wages for laborers lagged behind price increases. Thus severe famines frequently took place in the entire Nineteenth Century though the crop failures were localized.[4]

The following are the major famines in India under the British.

- 1770 Formidable Bengal Famine
- 1783 Madras Famine
- 1784 Famine in North India
- 1792 Bombay and Madras Famine
- 1803 Bombay Famine
- 1804 Famine in North India
- 1807 Madras Famine
- 1813 Bombay Famine
- 1837 Famine in North India
- 1854 Madras Famine
- 1860 Ganjam Famine and Baird Smith Report on this famine (1861)
- 1876-77 Great Famine in Madras, 1880 Famine Commission Report by Sir John Starchy.
- 1889 Madras Famine
- 1892 Famine in Madras, Bengal, Burma and Ajmer
- 1897 Famine in North India

- 1900 Famine in Punjab, Rajaputana, Central Provinces and Bombay

Source: 1. Romesh, C. Dutt, *Famines and Land Assessment in India,* rpt., Delhi, 1985, pp. 1-17.

2. Jean P. Draze, WIDER, Working Paper, p. 7a.

The bane of Nineteenth Century famines in India has been very aptly summarized by Baird Smith in his report when he wrote that Indian famines were "rather famines of work than of food; when work can be had and paid for, food is always forthcoming".[5] This idea is evident in almost all the subsequent Famine Commissions Reports like the one in 1880, submitted by Sir John Strachey, Sir John Lyall Commission of 1893 and McDonnell Commission of 1901.

The Famines brought havoc on agricultural laborers and rural artisans as they were the first victims. During severe famines cultivators became vulnerable to starvation in spite of the then widespread practice of storing large quantities of grain.[6] Another aspect of the Nineteenth Century famines is the view that scarcities occurred even in the midst of plenty and the Government did precious little in such context. Most of the literature on Nineteenth Century famines in India agree with the statement made by Lord George Hamilton [7] in 1902 which reads:

> What does a drought mean? It is not a question of food, the scarcity of food in a district affected by drought is the least of the evils with which the Government of India have to deal. There is nearly always a sufficiency of food in India to feed all the people within its limits; and owing to the development of the Railways, the British Government was able, no matter what part of the country may be affected, to pour in sufficient food to maintain the people of the district.[8]

There is great need to ascertain whether or not the absence of food availability problem during the Nineteenth Century famines in India was a myth projected by the successive famine Commissions. However, during the last two famines of the Century 1896-97 and 1900 there were massive crop failures throughout the country when the stocks were already diminishing.

In the backdrop of such intermittent famines which dot the entire Nineteenth Century India, an attempt is made in the following pages to see how a small region like Punganur Zamindari reacted to such drought and famines. It is also the purpose of this study to analyze the various relief measures, which were taken up during the periods of famines.

Notes

1. Sir James A. Murray ed., *A New English Dictionary -A Dictionary of Political economy (Palgrav)* p. 19.
2. L.C.A. Knowles, *Economic Development of British Overseas Empire*, Vol. I, p. 278.
3. H.S. Srivastava, *The history of Famines, 1858-1918,* Agra, 1968, p. 8.
4. Jean P. Dreze, "Famine Prevention in India," *Wider Working Paper* W.P 45, May 1989, Helsinki, pp. 7-8.
5. Col. Baird Smith, "Report of 14 August 1861". para 175 quoted in H.S. Srivastava, *The History of Indian Famines*, p. 53.
6. Famine Commission Report, quoted by J.P. Dreze, *Op.Cit.,* p. 9.
7. Statement of Sir George Hamilton, 3 February,1902, Quoted in J.P. Dreze, p. 71.

II

Historical Background

Punganur at present in Chittoor district of Andhra Pradesh was a prominent Zamindari in the Ceded Districts (now known as Rayalaseema area) in the Madras Presidency under the British rule. Situated above the Eastern Ghats in the north-west corner of Chittoor, Punganur is bounded by the kolar district of Karnataka State on the west, Madanapalle and Vayalpadu taluks on the north, Bangarupalem and Chandragiri on the east and Palamaner on the south. Punganur forms a part of the picturesque Mysore plateau region with an elevation of 2,000 to 2,500 feet above sea level. In its hey day, Punganur Zamindari extended over an area of 648 square miles covering 675 villages. Before it became a Zamindari, Punganur was the seat of powerful Palem for several centuries under successive Hindu and Muslim dynasties of south India. It came under the British occupation in 1799 after the defeat of Tipu Sultan in the Fourth Mysore war. Punganur was under the administrative jurisdiction of Cuddapah district, but transferred to the North Arcot district in 1856. It was in 1911 when Chittoor district was formed that Punganur came under the new district. The extent of the previous Zamindari is now constituted into a cluster of Mandals after the system of Talukas was dispensed with.

Punganur geographically falls into two divisions – the eastern division consisting of Chowdepalle, Sadum and Royalpet regions and the western division with Punganur, Ramasamudram and Muthukur firkas. The Eastern Ghats touch Punganur at its eastern borders at Avulapalle. From here, the ranges extend up to Tirupati hills on which the famous hill temple of Sri Venkateswara is situated. There are a number of hill ranges all over Punganur region. Punganur forests are mainly of two types. They are Tropical dry deciduous forests and Tropical thorn forests. At present these forests come under Class III reserved Forest lands, but under the erstwhile Zamindari administration, they were all private forests under the direct control of the Zamindar. These forests had plenty of Bamboo and yielded a lot of timber that was used for agricultural implements and for the building of houses. The shrubs were cut for fuel and the leaves were used as green manure. Punganur jungles also provided extensive pasture- lands and for this very reason, the area came to be known for its special breed of cows, known as *Punganur Breed.*

The monsoon has been always less favorable to Punganur as the area obviously does not lie within the north-west or south-east monsoon zones, though it depends very precariously on both the monsoons. The average rainfall is a mere 73.66 cms. In Punganur, there are a number of small rivers which drain the waters from the hills. *Pincha*, and *Kaundinya* are the two main rivers in the Punganur Taluk which join the Bahuda and Palar rivers respectively. The Palar basin, which is a deep ravine is about 10 km north west of Punganur town.

There are no natural lakes or springs in Punganur. The only sources for irrigation therefore are tanks and wells besides the river channels. The streams that collect rain water from the hill slopes are embanked at favorable points to form series of tanks. There are more than 1,200 tanks spread over the entire Punganur taluk; but this includes a large number of puddles – percolation tanks and very small tanks the *ayacut* of which does not exceed 20 acres. The largest of the tanks in Punganur is the Sankar Royalpet tank built by the Zamindar, Shankar Royal I (1781-1830), which irrigates about 1,200 acres. The total number of wells used for irrigation in the Punganur taluk are estimated to be about 1,147.

Though there were no minerals worthy to be mentioned here, iron-sand was collected in considerable amount in the hill streams of the Zamindari. A. F. Cox, the compiler of the *Manual of North Arcot District*, has testified that the quality of the iron available here was so good that it was generally preferred to that of even the imported one. The plough- shares made of the locally available iron were generally sold at the Chowdepalle weekly Shandy. Cox also speaks of the sturdy bill-hooks made out of the local iron. No further survey of the mineral resources in the taluk have been made after Cox's report in 1881.

The soils all over Punganur are generally light loamy with red sand. Therefore they are less fertile than the adjoining taluks like Palamaner, Madanapalle and Vayalpadu. Wet crops like paddy and sugarcane are cultivated under the tanks and wells, where there were assured irrigational facilities. Ground-nut is a major crop in the vast dry belts. The other principal crops are Ragi, Jowar, Bajra, Maize, Korra,(Fox Tail Millet) Horse-gram, Black- gram, Red-gram, Chillies etc. Orchards, growing fruits like Mango, Citrus, Banana are found in few parts of the taluk. Though the staple food of the people here is rice, Ragi is in extensive use.

Lack of perennial sources of irrigation, unfavorable monsoons, poor soils, lack of natural resources, absence of adequate transport facilities have all made Punganur a backward region even by the Rayalaseema standards. While there was not much change in the production of food grains, there was a perceptible increase in the population over the years.

Early History of the Zamindari

Before it was constituted into a Zamindari, Punganur was the seat of a powerful Palem for several centuries under successive dynasties of south India. At a time when the British power itself was yet to strike roots in this part of the country and also when the neighboring Palems were turbulent and restive, the Punganur Palegars supported the British for which Punganur Palegars were rewarded with a raised status as Zamindari.

Punganur Zamindari had a hoary past. A number of inscriptions found in and around Punganur testifies the ancient history of this area. This area was a part of the kingdoms ruled by various dynasties as the ancient temple at Laddigam is a testimony to the rule of Cholas in this area. There are also a number of sites of historical importance all over the taluk that tell in fragments the history of this place. The establishment of the Vijayanagar empire marks an important epoch in the history of this region. During the two centuries of their rule, the Vijayanagar kings subdued the turbulent Palegars and Punganur also thus was brought under the Vijayanagar rulers. The Palegars were entrusted with the task of collecting the land revenue, maintenance of law and order, and help strengthen the imperial power. But after the fall of the Vijayanagar kingdom in 1565, the Nawabs of Golconda as the Subehdars of the Deccan under the Mughals, held sway over the entire south-India. Punganur formed a part of the Gurramkonda Pargana and Gurramkonda itself was placed under the Nawab of Cuddapah who in turn was under the authority of the Golconda Sultan.

In 1757 when the Marathas defeated Cuddapah Nawab, Punganur came under their rule. But after Hyder Ali rose to power in Mysore in the year, 1761, he wrested Gurramkonda from the Marathas. Hyder even married a Gurramkonda princess, Fakhr -un- nisa, and of this union was born the famed Tipu Sultan. Tipu inherited Hyder's kingdom in 1782. After the defeat and the death of Tipu Sultan in 1799, during the fourth Mysore War, the British took over several tracts of land which included even Punganur.

When the Ceded Districts were transferred to the British in 1800 by the Nizam of Hyderabad as a result of the Subsidiary Alliance System, the Palegar of Punganur was directed to remit the peishcush to the newly appointed Principal Collector, Thomas Munro. Thus Punganur finally came under the control of the Company administration. The Punganur chiefs distinguished themselves with their loyalty and punctuality in paying the peishcush, for which they were duly rewarded by the British authorities with titles and honors. It was in 1861 that the status of Punganur was raised from the position of a Palem to that of the Zamindari when Shankar Royal, the then Palegar was granted the *Sanad -I -Milkedt –Istimrar* or deed of permanent settlement wherein it was stated that the Zamindari was granted to the Zamindar, "his heirs or successors on perpetuity".

Punganur Under the British

The British relations with Punganur Zamindari were based on the twin principles of exercise of authority and expectancy of obedience. The concluding words in the formal letters addressed by the Provincial Governors or even the District Collectors, like "Keep regard" or "remain satisfied" amply testifies this nature of relationship. The government's interest in preferring one claimant to the other as the prospective Zamindar and in installing a claimant on the *gaddi* was based on ensuring such loyalty and obedience from the Zamindar. The system of permanent settlement envisaged the perpetuation of the hereditary principle as regards the succession of the Zamindars.

While the Zamindar was expected to serve as an effective link between the Government on one side and the people on the other, sufficient care was taken in matters of succession of the Zamindars.

The administrative system of Punganur, which was based mainly on the personal preferences of the individual Zamindar, underwent changes under the British. His military was disbanded and his powers over his subjects were curtailed. He was made amenable to law. From 1799 to 1833 the Zamindari was under the overall control of the District Collector and the Zamindar was treated as an employee of the British . He was assigned to collect revenues on a remuneration of 20 percent of the total rent. But after 1833 the Zamindar was exempted from the obligation of subjecting his accounts for the scrutiny of the Government. He was treated as the de facto administrator as he was vested with the powers to grant pattas in his name. He was issued permanent Sannad in 1861 and thus he became the *de jure* administrator as the Government gave him every power relating to revenue matters.

The mode of land control generally affects the economic conditions of the people in the given area, where land happens to be the sole source of livelihood. The ryots in the Zamindari held the lands on pattas. The cultivable lands were classified and assessed on Taram basis. For purposes of rent collection, lands were divided into several categories and the assessment of rent on each category of land varied. There were extensive Inam lands in the Zamindari. The rate of rent on Inams was 50 percent of the total assessment. When such Inams were resumed by the Government or relinquished by the Inamdars, they ceased to be Inams.

The Tenural Structures as prevailed in Punganur Zamindari were not favorable for the peasants This coupled with heavy peishcush that the Zamindar was to pay to the Government, interfered with the agricultural growth in the area. The total cultivable area did not vary much under the British. Irrigation remained a major constraint for agricultural development and this in turn made the entire area prone to frequent famines and scarcities.

III

Land Tenures and Revenue Settlements

Unfavorable land tenures, unjust revenue settlements and excessive tax rates generally play a significant role in deciding the level of economic performance of the given region, particularly in the agrarian economy and add to the severity of famines and scarcities. The prosperity or otherwise of the peasantry largely depends on the terms and conditions with which the lands are held. This was true in the case of the Punganur Zamindari during the 19th. century. There were various types of land tenures and varieties of occupancy rights of the peasants. Punganur had the distinction of possessing a large number of Inams which were free gifts of lands held by peasants on easy terms of settlements. The enfranchisement of these Inams by the Inam Commission (1858) resulted in changes in the tenural structures of such lands. An attempt is made in this chapter to describe the various types of land holdings and tenural rights the peasants in the Zamindari possessed.

The land holdings in the Zamindari were broadly divided into two divisions: 1. Occupied or Settled lands and 2. Unoccupied or Unsettled lands.

I. Settled Lands:

The Settled or Occupied lands were generally those on which the *Teerva*[1] or rent was settled or fixed and on which assets of the concerned estate were calculated. The ownership rights of such lands remained with the *ryot* which he cultivated himself or sublet. He might also transfer the land by sale, gift or mortgage or he may relinquish by resignation at will. If the fixed Teerva on any land happened to be high, the Zamindar on representation, could reduce it. But this rent known as *Cowle Teerva,* (contract rent), did not hold good with the successor Zamindar. The new Zamindar may continue with the Cowle Teerva or may raise it again to the usual settled rates. The Settled lands were mainly of three types; A. *Khalesa* or Circar Lands, B. *Khanigi* or Zamindar's personal lands and C. *Inam* Lands.

A. *Khalesa Lands*

All the cultivable lands assigned to the ryots on fixed rents were known as Khalesa or Circar lands. The holders of these lands were known as *Pattadars.*[2] who as proprietors, personally cultivated these lands. Rich land holders generally sub-let their lands to the needy ryots.

Unlike other Zamindaries in Andhra, Punganur had its survey conducted by Thomas Munro, as early as 1802-07 when he was the Principal Collector of the Ceded Districts. As survey was an essential feature of the Ryotwari settlement, Munro made it a point to conduct survey as well as settlement before fixing the *Theerva* (rent). He made the Zamindar responsible for the collection of rents on a remuneration of 20 percent for himself.

During the survey, lands were classified and assessed on Tharam[3] basis with a broad classification as Wet, Dry and Garden lands. The wet lands were sub divided into five or six classes and dry were divided into eight or nine classes. However, garden lands had no sub classes and were treated as one class. The assessment on each Tharam of land was arrived at by taking into consideration the opinion of the local inhabitants. In arriving at the decision, apart from the productive power of the soil, the continuity of the irrigational facilities, proximity to markets, facilities of transport and such other local circumstances were also taken into account. Immediately after the survey was done, each village was furnished with a map showing the position of each traverse survey and boundary marks that have been erected. Fields of irregular shape were measured into rectangular plots. The village officials were responsible for the careful maintenance of the survey mark-stones. Sometimes these mark stones are clandestinely removed or counterfeited but such acts of mischief were soon discovered as the villagers always watched them zealously as they all had high stakes on such markings. Along the frontier between Punganur and Mysore territory, the survey marks planted by Thomas Munro bore representations of the sun and moon reflecting the local sensibilities. They were locally known as "Sasanams" and were engraved on large boulders or on small granite stones, buried in the ground where rocks do not occur.[4] There granite stone markings were treated with great respect by the ryots as they were the ones planted by the government personnel at the behest of the Collector. At many places, such prominent survey stones go with the name "Munro Stone" even at this distance of time.

The rent paid by the Pattadars (land owners) to the Zamindar was in cash. The commutation of rent from kind to cash as existed in the northern Circars, did not happen in Punganur[5]. A study conducted in 1916 in Thettupalle village in Punganur Zamindari which paid an annual revenue of Rs. 622 -5-2 provides a representative picture of the rates of land rents in the Zamindari. The study revealed that wet lands of the village were of six grades and dry lands were of five grades while the Inam lands were of four grades. The assessment rate of the first grade in wet land was Rs. 8-14-3. per acre, while that of the dry land was Rs. 2-1-9. But in the statement submitted by the Zamindar to the Prakasham Committee in 1938, the lands were shown to be of four types. They were dry, wet, dry garden, and wet garden. The dry lands were shown to be of 45 grades, wet lands were of 30 grades, dry garden of 33 grades and wet garden of 28 grades. The assessment on each grade in each type varied greatly. The maximum and minimum rates on dry-lands varied from Rs. 4-7-2 to Rs. 0-11-10, on dry garden-lands from Rs. 12-3-7 to Rs. 0-11-10 and wet garden lands from Rs. 17-12-6 to Rs. 2-3-6.[6]

If the peasant proprietor did not cultivate himself, his lands were sublet on sharecropping. Under this system, the land owner himself paid the land revenue and other cesses to the Zamindar. The sub- tenant bore all the cost of all the inputs. The produce was equally shared between the land holder and the cultivator. The hay or the straw was generally taken by the cultivator. In cultivating crops like *Paddy, Ragi, Cholam, Maize* and others, half the produce went to the cultivator, but in the case of Sugarcane, the cultivator got one and a half of the share while the Pattadar got one share. In case the Pattadar supplied a pair of bulls to plough the land, one sixth of the produce and if two pairs were supplied, one eighth of the produce was given to the cultivator[7]. This system of sharecropping is an age-old practice and the contract between the cultivator and the sub-tenant was purely based on custom. It had no legal validity as it was done through oral agreements. How these customary shares eluded the grasp of the most perceptive economists is illustrated by Rothermund when he writes:

> Customary rent is therefore, in every respect different from the kind of rent about which Ricardo said that it does not interfere with prices but is influenced by them. In fact,

Ricardo's dictum may be reversed in the case of customary rents.[8]

Dharma Kumar's argument on the subject is more or less on these lines: the income of the poorest sharecropper and the agricultural laborer is almost the same, and there is no great difference in their economic functions.[9] But when seen in the context of land relations in the village communities, the sharecropper was more secure than the laborer who got a daily wage. The former had his own cattle, implements and access to inputs. He had fair credit worthiness from the village money-lender and he was a *Ryot* in the local hierarchy. The landless agricultural laborer never had these advantages in the village.

B. Khanigi Lands

Another category of settled lands was the *Khanigi,* or Zamindar's personal lands. These lands were spread all over the Zamindari with the Zamindar having at least a few acres of land practically in every major village. These lands were given by the Zamindar to the cultivators on sharecropping or on rent. But the lands adjacent to the *Kasba,* (main village i.e. Punganur)), the lands were cultivated by the Zamindar by employing his own laborers. The total annual demand on the Khanigi lands for example, in 1934-35 amounted to Rs. 39,706-13-4. Like some of the Zamindars of Northern Circars, the Punganur Zamindars also occupied large tracts of lands belonging to the poor ryots of the area.

C. Inams

The word 'Inam' literally means, a gift or reward. Wilson's glossary defines the term Inam as a gift or benefaction conferred by a grantor on a grantee. In some cases the grants made with no specific reference to perpetuity also came under Inams. While Jagir was a political grant which implied conditions of service, the Inams were smaller personal grants with no such conditions.[10] Sir Charles Travelyan, Governor of Madras during 1859-60, in his Minutes on Inams dated 13 May, 1859 designated them as the "Madras Tax Free Tenures".

The origin of Inams could be traced to the remote past in South India. The gift of land is enjoined by the Hindu Sastras as the most meritorious of the charities and therefore every Hindu king was ambitious of distinguishing his reign by the extent and value of lands he granted as Inams.

The contributions made by the Inam tenures has been assessed by scholars from various angles. The views of Robert Frykenberg and Eric Stokes in this regard are very significant. Frykenberg argued that the Inams were tools in the rise of Indian Imperial system. He stated that:

> The Silent Settlement (the Inams according to him were silent settlements) was an important component in the constitution of the British Raj in South India – a constitution depending heavily upon a silent consensus between the Government and the governed.[11]

Frykenberg's concept of Inam as 'Silent Settlement' and that there was silent consensus between the Government and the governed is based on the fact that there was always the discretion of the government in fixing the rent on the Inams. His division of Inams in the Madras Presidency into four categories is highly convincing. It should also be remembered that every village was on the lines of a corporate self sufficient unit comprising within itself the entire machinery of local economic functioning. Eric Stokes on the other hand has assessed that the Inams in South India were "devices for encouraging colonization rather than one to escape the revenue demand".[12] A Perusal of all the 422 different Inam tenures prevalent in the Madras Presidency will convince that the original grantors of Inams meant them to play an effective role in making villages socially viable and economically self sufficient units.

Of the 675 hamlets in Punganur Zamindari, 442 hamlets were under the control of the Collector at the time when Punganur came under the British, The remaining 233 hamlets were Inams. The most important types of these Inams were as follows:

TABLE- 3.1

Type of Inams	*No. hamlets*
Amara Muktha	43
Amara Charane	96
Naukeresh	15
Shotriums	51
Sarva Inams	28
Total Inam hamlets	233

Source: General Reports of the BOR, 1815, .64.

1. *Amaram Inams*

The word Amaram[13] means 'easy' and therefore, this tenure was considered to be a favorable one. Amaram grants were generally held by the armed retainers of the Palegar. A grantee of Amaram Inam was bound to attend on the grantor and any neglect or delay in discharging his duty was punished by dispossession from the Inam. In case an Inamdar could not attend to his assigned duties in person, he should provide an efficient substitute in his place. The Amaram Inamdars were entitled to extra allowance while on duty. The Amaram Inams were held on hereditary basis. However, the grants were resumable when the holder failed to attend his duties. But when an Inamdar distinguished himself, particularly in a battle, he was handsomely rewarded [14]

The total number of grantees of Amaram Inams in the Punganur Zamindari in 1800 was 1844. Out of them, 108 were Duffadars or *Daladhipathis* and the remaining were ordinary peons.[15] These Inams were assigned in different methods. In few cases, the villages as a whole were given to the Inamdars who paid the Circar rent and appropriated the rest for their own use. Such Inams were known as Major Inams. Another method was the grant of detached pieces of Inams in different villages and these were known as Minor Inams.[16]

The Amaram villages were divided into Amarmuktha and Amaram Char Ane. The rent on Amarmuktha was fixed and did not change under any circumstance. But in Amar Char Ane, rent was fixed every year according to cultivation and 25 percent of the net produce was paid to the Circar. In both the cases, the Inamdars were the cultivators. Duffadars were the heads of the villages to whom the pattas were granted by the Collector.[17] After the military establishment was disbanded in Punganur, the Amaram Inams were brought under *Kattubadis*.

2. *Kattubadi Inams*

The Kattubadi Inams were granted on tenure of service at a fixed, invariable and favorable rent by the Palegars or Zamindars to their armed servants and personal retainers. The Kattubadi Inamdars were inferior to the Amarakars and were liable to frequent service. Though theoretically they were expected to perform military service to the chief when called upon, it cannot be said that all of them belonged to the military profession. A good number of them were domestic employees of the Zamindars. Kattubadi peons who enjoyed Amaram villages after the dispossession of the Amarakars in Punganur. They were also employed by the Zamindar "for collection of kisths, for furnishing customary guards in Ghats for prevention of highway robbery and murders and for forming the usual guards at the Palace, fort etc."[18]

The duties and functions of the Kattubadidars were so vague and varied that the Collector summoned all such Kattubadidars in 1813 for physical verification to Madanapalle, 20 km. away, where he was camping. It is to be noted that all of them immediately collected themselves before the Collector leaving their stations and causing no inconvenience whatsoever and making the Collector to be convinced that they were not performing any effective service. Yet, as the police duties were carried by the Kattubadidars under the management of the Zamindar, he allowed them on the condition that they should be ascribed more active duties. When a separate police force was organized in the Zamindari by 1867, Kattubadi set up became superfluous and so it was dispensed with.[19]

The Kattubadi Inam lands were generally of poor quality and depended largely on rain. The returns therefore were meager and were not sufficient even to meet the rent.[20] As service obligations made the Kattubadi Inamdars to be absent from the lands frequently, they were forced to let their lands to others for cultivation. As a result, the assessments on such Inam lands were generally high.

3. *Naukerpesh*

The Naukerpesh Villages were held by the dependants of the Zamindar on grants given by him[21] or his ancestors. In Punganur there were 23 Naukerpesh villages of which Thomas Munro continued 15 and directed the remaining 8 to be sequestered. Out of the 15 in the list, 4 were held by the Samprathis, 4 by Vakils in the service of the Zamindar, 5 by Zamindar, 5 by Zamindar's *Rajabhandhus* (relatives), 1 by the family doctor and another by the Khazi of Punganur. The Board of Revenue in their circular Instructions of 15 October, 1799, held the view that the Naukerpesh Inam lands were exempted from public revenue.[22] The Board also stated clearly that all private lands appropriated by the Zamindars or other land holders and all lands held by private servants of the Zamindar were considered as part of the Circar lands and were responsible for public revenue. In 1814 however the Collector of Cuddapah wrote to the Board that the Naukerpesh villages in Punganur to be continued under the respective Inamdars. But many of these Inams were resumed by the Inam Commission which was set up in 1858 by the government of Madras.

4. *Shotriums*

Originally, Shotrium grants were made only to Brahmins well versed in Vedas. In Punganur there were 53 Shotrium hamlets whose value of land under cultivation was estimated in 1830 to be Pagodas 2,558. The duties of the Brahmins and other family priests (Jangams) who enjoyed the Shotrium villages were to "explain the Sastras, to perform ceremonies, and officiate at the usual feasts and festivals" according to the custom of the Zamindari.

5. *Sarva Inams*

The Sarva Inams were those that were held free of all assessment. These Inams were also known as *Ekabhogyam* Inams or *Agraharams*. This category of Inams was granted to religious and charitable institutions like the temples, chowltries, Dharmasalas and water pandals etc. and also to religious and pious persons. In the entire Punganur Zamindari there were 28 Sarva Inams which were completely free from land tax.

Besides the above, there were other Inams in Punganur like Kattugutta lands. These Inams were held at a fixed money rent usually less than the full assessment. As this kind of grant was also made in return for military service, it was granted under the usual Kattubadi Inams. The *Thoti, Thalari, Neergatti,* Washer man, Shepherd, Cobbler etc. who rendered service to the village, were all remunerated partly by the Inam grants and partly by payment either in kind or in cash. For their services they were also remunerated by the individual ryots by Merah (a small portion from the produce), cooked food given daily or annual cash payment.

2. *Unsettled Lands*

Unsettled lands were unoccupied lands or unassigned common lands or waste lands on which the government did not compute any rent in fixing the peishcush the Zamindar was to pay. In practice, these waste lands formed an important source of income for the Zamindar. The proprietary rights on these lands rested with the Zamindar till he gave them away to the ryots on assignment. The method of assignment of waste lands was generally as follows; When a ryot was willing to cultivate any tract of waste land, it was given to him on cowle for a term of few years. On the expiry of the period of cowle, a fixed theerva was settled on the basis of the valuation of that land by the government servants – the Karnam and Moniyagar of the village. The amount thus fixed was called *Mamool Theerva,* (usual rent) and it would be entered in the account books with the Karnam. Such lands were generally not relinquished by the ryots as they were considered valuable properties and the tenure, a superior one.

The unsettled lands were of two types: 1. The Paramboke, or waste lands and 2. Tank-bed lands.

1. *Purumboke Lands*

The value of the total arable Paramboke lands in the Zamindari was estimated in the first survey (1802- 1807) at Controy Pagodas (C.P)71,958. The entire Paramboke in the Zamindari at that time was divided into two groups: Anadi Banjar i.e. land lying waste for twenty years or more., and the leag Banjar, waste land fit for cultivation. The former was valued at CP 40,553 and the latter at CP 31,405. As the total land estimated to be under cultivation was CP 57,352, the waste land of both categories alone was 120 percent more than the arable lands in the Zamindari. Usually the ryots changed their lands periodically to occupy fresh wastes in order to allow the lands which were impoverished by constant use to recover by allowing them to remain fallow for few years.[23] In this context, Thomas Munro, the Principal Collector, wrote in 1802 thus:

> ....increase of cultivation cannot be regarded as such when taken into general account of the whole country for they are not more than the equivalent of that proportion of the cultivated land which the ryots every year throw up in order to occupy fallow and waste.[24]

The Board of Revenue was of the opinion that *Anadi Banjar* in Punganur Zamindari was fit to be defined not merely as land laid waste for more than twenty years, but as " land not cultivated within the memory of men, not likely to be within any period to be now fixed"[25] However, when the decennial lease introduced in the Zamindari in 1814, all the Paramboke lands were included in the assets.

The wastelands near towns and cities were valuable for building purposes but they were generally of no value in the dry regions except for pasturage in favorable seasons. The Board with a view to discourage the usual tendency of the cultivators to occupy waste lands in order to avoid payment of higher rents felt that the cultivator with the limited capital, livestock and labour available should concentrate on the cultivation of normal lands rather than moving into waste lands. [26] The Board cited in this context, the condition in the estates of Salem and Chengalpattu Districts where waste lands were taken into consideration when the land revenue was permanently settled on the Muttadars and those lands were never occupied for several years. Therefore the Board of Revenue felt:

> It would not be prudent to look to any benefit to be derived from the waste lands of Punganur within any period that it would be at all useful to name.[27]

A large amount of waste lands remained unoccupied in the Punganur Zamindari. The Paramboke lands were generally near the foot of the hills and jungles, far away from the villages and were covered with stones and shrubs. The occupation and cultivation of these lands was not very easy. That explains why nearly 75 percent of such lands were lying unoccupied.

> The ill paid Pyamshidars or Surveyors conducted the survey and imposed the assessment on lands in a most irregular and shabby way that the results were most inaccurate and untrustworthy.[28]

In the memorandum submitted to the Prakasam Committee in January, 1938, the Zamindar stated that the 'waste lands' have not been defined even in the revised Estate lands Act of 1908 and that there had been assignment of Banjar lands in Punganur Zamindari.[29]

2. *Tank-Bed Lands*

Another type of land from which the Zamindar derived revenue was the tank bed lands. The term tank-bed was used to denote the lands within the water spread of a tank that is intended to hold the water necessary for irrigating the lands under its ayakat. The tank bed lands were cultivated when the tank remained dry for a number of years. But such cultivation would not make them *Ryothi* lands, so as to hold permanent *patta* or the title. [30] These lands were also not defined in the Estate land Act of 1908. They were not treated as community

Paramboke either. As the Sanad given to the Zamindar stated that he was the sole proprietor of all lands in the Zamindari, he was thus entitled to the proprietary rights of all the extensive Tank bed lands in the Zamindari as well.[31]

Most of the tanks in the Punganur Zamindari were Dasabandam tanks which were maintained by the Dasabandamdars, who generally objected to the assigning of tank bed lands on the ground that such assigning would affect the proper maintenance of the tank bunds. This accounted for the low rate of tank bed assignments in the Zamindari. Even though the Zamindar had every right to assign the tank bed lands for cultivation on a cowle assignment, in general, they were not assigned. If assigned, such numbers were very less.

The tenural structures in Punganur Zamindari to a very large extent were influenced by the Ryotwari principles introduced by Thomas Munro. The Survey and settlement that he conducted prevented the Zamindar from collecting land rents more than that was generally due. The waste lands which normally were great assets to the Zamindars elsewhere in the Presidency, were not so in Punganur because of the poor quality of the soils. The Inam Commission that was established came heavily on the prevalence of a large number of Inams and suggested resuming them. The resumed Inams were given over to the Zamindar on a remuneration of one third of the collection of revenue. The ryots in general were insulated from any possible harassment from the Zamindar and his officials because of the tenural rights they were allowed to enjoy from the beginning of the British authority.

Revenue Settlements

Closely related to land tenures is the revenue settlements in the Zamindari that reflect the rural economy of the populations depending on agriculture. The revenue collections also determine the vulnerability of the agricultural populations to fall victims to scarcities and famines during times of drought. There were a number of stages in which the British made settlements with the Zamindars in Punganur Zamindari. An attempt is made in this section to discuss those stages and their impact on the agricultural population.

It is to be noted that in the case of the Zamindars elsewhere in Andhra, either permanent Sanads were issued or the Zamindaries were altogether dispossessed, in the case of Punganur, temporary settlements of varying durations were made till 1861 when a Sanad was finally granted. The uncertainty in such fixation of the peishcush amounts naturally had its cascading effects on the peasants and in their paying rents to the Zamindar. The severity of the successive famines in the Zamindari to an extent was also due to this uncertainty, the heavy rates of land rents and denial of any remissions during unfavorable seasons.

At the time when Punganur came under the British occupation, the Company administration was seized with idea of extending the system of Permanent Settlement even to Madras Presidency on the same lines as was introduced in Bengal by the then Governor General, Lord Cornwallis in 1793.[32] It was the firm belief of Cornwallis that the British East India Company would secure for itself "all the substantial advantages of their revenue and commerce."[33] The Court of Directors were also convinced of the advantages of Cornwallis' Settlement and desired that the Bengal Revenue System be introduced in the Madras Presidency also. Accordingly, the Governor of Madras, Edward Clive issued Permanent Sanads to all the Zamindars. Even the Western Palems namely Venkatagiri in Nellore, Kalahasti and Karvetinagar in Chittoor District, and Sydapur in Chengalpattu District (now in Tamil Nadu), were also settled on permanent basis in 1802 and Sanads were issued to them. However, Punganur Zamindari was kept under periodical leases of varying durations for nearly sixty years till 1861 when the *Sanad-e-Milkeut Isthmrar* or Deed of Permanent Settlement was granted to the Zamindar.[34]

Principal Collector of Ceded Districts (1800-1807) to which Punganur belonged, was the main reason for the inordinate delay in granting of the permanent Sanad to the Zamindar[35]. Munro being a strong advocate of the Ryotwari Settlement, did not favor settling it on a permanent basis like all other neighboring Zamindaries.

Munro's Settlement: Ryotwari

At the time when Punganur was being transferred to the Ceded Districts by 1803, Thomas Munro was experimenting with the Ryotwari system of land settlement which later earned him a unique place in the history of the land settlements in India. The distinguishing feature of the Ryotwari was that the government came in direct contact with the ryot and land revenue was collected through its own personnel without the interference of the intermediary like the Zamindar. Munro was thus an opponent of the Permanent Settlement and he tried his best to stop that system being implemented in Punganur. He wrote to the Board of Revenue that he would settle the revenues of Punganur on the same lines as was done in the case of other Palegars in the Ceded Districts. He wrote:

> As the Palegar (of Punganur) now belongs to the Ceded Districts, the terms which he may obtain will attract the attention of the neighboring Palegars of Gurramkondah and excite discontentment among them if they are more favorable than their own. ....I could therefore wish to be at liberty to settle with him in the same manner as I have done with

> them…That is to say, by investigating the produce, allowing him about one fifth of the net revenue.[36]

Munro took meticulous care in collecting information as regards the produce of Punganur as well as the peishcush the successive Palegars paid to their suzerains earlier. He personally perused through the records and Sanads in possession of the Zamindar with great caution to ascertain facts. Munro studied the peishcush amounts Punganur paid from the time when it was under the Golconda Nawabs, under the Nawabs of Cuddapah, under the Marathas, Hyder Ali and under Tipu Sultan. Munro's report came to the conclusion that the amount 20,000 pagodas fixed in 1799, jointly by the Company and the Mysore kingdom after the fall of Tipu Sultan to be the final amount that the Zamindar was to pay annually.[37] Further, Munro also pointed out that he could not dispense with Punganur as he did with the rest of such Palems in the Ceded Districts. He wrote to the Board thus:

> The Palegar of Punganur had held his District for some years on easy terms of peishcush. The possession of it had also been virtually confirmed to him by the decision respecting the disputed villages of Chadum and Cundoor. I could not therefore reduce him exactly to the level of the Palegars who properly belonged to the Ceded Districts.[38]

Thomas Munro did not make individual Ryotwari settlement in Punganur for the year 1802-03, but only *Kulwar* or Village Settlement. He gave the village heads Pattas in the name of the Company and not in the name of the Palegar. The Palegar was allowed one-fifth of the total amount of assessment as remuneration for collecting the revenues. Before he was transferred away from the Ceded Districts in1807, Munro made periodic visits to Punganur and caused the survey of the entire Zamindari and even fixed *Paimash* numbers as in the Ryotwari tracts.[39] The total assessment of each field and village in the entire Zamindari was recorded in a separate account called *Tarwar*. In one of his visits to Punganur, Munro checked several village accounts himself and resumed the Inams granted liberally by the Zamindar. Munro did not consult the Palegar in the matters of survey and assessment and also in the preparation of Paimash and Tarwar accounts. When the Palegar raised fears over the heavy rents due to survey, Munro informed him that "the intention of survey was only to decrease the rates rather than to increase".[40]

A close examination of the accounts of valuation reports of Punganur as stated in the survey Reports of Munro and the actual collections made during the period when he was the Collector, reveals that Munro's assessment of lands in Punganur was much higher than the actual collections. Such heavy rents collected by the British almost from the beginning of their rule, was also a reason for the poverty of the peasants and even a small drought was enough for the famine to set in.

Thomas Munro introduced in Punganur a peculiar system which was unique in more than one way. He did not dispense with the Palegar as he did in the case of other Palegars in the Ceded Districts. At the same time, he did not recognize the Palegar as the proprietor of all lands in the Palem. Instead of fixing the permanent peishcush as it is normally done in other Zamindaries, the Punganur Zamindar was asked to collect the revenues on behalf of the government and was allowed one-fifth of the total assessment as his allowance. The Munro system in Punganur contained all the principles of the Ryotwari system but with the Palegar as the head of the Palem.

Settlements Under the Later Collectors

Thomas Munro was succeeded by W.H. Chaplin as the Collector of Ceded Districts in 1807. Shankar Royal I, the Palegar of Punganur petitioned the Collector to get Punganur settled on a permanent basis. He sent a Vakil, Venkata Rao, with a memorial to request the Collector to take up the matter with the Board of Revenue.[41] Chaplin in turn addressed a letter to the Board of Revenue suggesting that a Permanent Settlement should be made with the Palegar and that the Palegar be free from the interference of the government. [42] He further suggested that it could be raised to either 29,000 or 30,000 pagodas; but in any case it should never be below pagodas 29,000. The Board in reply suggested that a thorough examination of the matter should be made before deciding on the Permanent Settlement. The Board wrote:

> On deciding upon a subject of such importance as the Permanent Settlement of a considerable Zamindari, it is necessary that it should undergo a full examination and that a formal report should be submitted for the ultimate determination of the Government.[43]

The Board directed the Collector to report on the petition of the Palegar, pending that it was decided that the annual lease settlements should be continued. The Board also reassured the Palegar that the proposed arrangement would not preclude the adoption of permanent settlement at any period of lease.[44] When Robert Ross succeeded Chaplin as the Principal Collector in 1811, Punganur along with other areas of the District, was under the Triennial Settlement introduced by Traverse, who for a brief period officiated as the Principal Collector before Ross took over. This system was considered by Ross as adverse to both the Palegar and for the government, and so he discontinued it and reverted to annual settlement.[45] Ross after examining all the relevant records, reported in August 1811, that the Palegar was rightful incumbent of the Zamindari as he was invested duly by Hyder Ali of Mysore in 1781. As far as the value of the Zamindari was concerned, he wondered whether Munro's assessment was right. He felt that the assessment was so high that the Palegar was never able to pay them at any time.

Ross did not prefer to accept the suggestion of Chaplin in fixing the lease of Punganur at pagodas 29,000 on the ground that a lease should never be fixed in an arbitrary manner. He argued that it was not what Punganur had paid, but what it could pay should be the criteria in deciding the settlement amount for future. He therefore suggested that the average of land rent collected in Punganur during the preceding seven years from 1804 to 1811, should be taken into consideration while fixing the peishcush. Based on the statistics, Ross fixed the annual peishcush at Pagodas 28,000. He also suggested that the Palegar be given permanent settlement immediately. Ross felt that Munro introduced Ryotwari Settlement in 1802 as a matter of his general principle and not because of any lapse on the part of the Palegar. He also felt that the revenues would be more reassured to the government and could be easily collected if only a permanent peishcush was fixed than on the lease settlements. He further concluded that it was most "advantageous, most gracious and most just" to fix permanent peishcush on Punganur.[46]

His views on permanently fixing the peishcush were strengthened when on a personal visit to Punganur, he was, in his own words "much disheartened to see that cultivation was badly affected throughout Punganur".[47] This according to him *was more due to the uncertainty of the settlement than due to the failure of rains*. It is to be noted that the frequent scarcities and famines in the Zamindari were not only because of the drought as generally believed to be, but also because of the uncertainty of settlement and the temporary leases to which the Zamindar was subjected to a protracted period, though the Collector Robert Ross strongly recommended for the granting of permanent settlement. If that was not possible immediately, he wanted that the Board may allow him to make annual settlement for that year alone.[48] The Board permitted to make such annual settlement not only for that year (1811) but even for the subsequent year as the subject was of great importance and an immediate decision was not possible.

After the annual settlements for those two years, Robert Ross in 1813 suggested to the Board that the economic conditions in the Zamindari were such that even the earlier amount he suggested i.e. 28,000 pagodas was a heavy amount on the part of the Zamindar and opined that it should be lower than the said amount. He stated that due to the close proximity to the villages in Mysore, the lands in Punganur were cultivated on terms far below the survey rates. He narrated how the failure of rains caused great exodus of the ryots to Mysore and when they returned on improvement of the season, it was not before a considerable portion of ploughing was over.[49] The observation of Ross is significant as the migration of poorer sections to the Mysore region for work was due to uncertainty of the periodical assessments in the Zamindari.

Robert Ross thus differed from the decision of Thomas Munro and suggested that a permanent peishcush on Punganur to be settled forthwith at a much lower than what he himself had suggested earlier. He also suggested that the Zamindar be given a higher percentage of remuneration at thirty three and a half percent and not 20% as suggested by Munro. But the Board still was in no mood to settle Punganur revenues on a permanent basis. Because of the repeated requests of the Collector, the Board of revenue wanted the Collector to make a Decennial Settlement instead of annual settlement.

Decennial Settlement (1814-23)

The next mode of revenue settlement that Punganur was subjected to by the Company Government at Madras was the

Ten Year Settlement, popularly known as the Decennial Settlement. As per the directive of the Board of Revenue, Ross, the Collector settled Punganur's revenues on Decennial lease system in 1814. The details of the settlement for the entire period, 1814 to 1823 were sent to the Palegar in which Ross informed that the *Inamdars* i.e. leasees were to pay the stipulated amounts to the government every year. The Palegar was asked to cooperate with the leases and collect as usual from the leases on an allowance of one-fifth of the total collections and should not collect anything more than what it was stipulated.[50]

The Decennial lease, contrary to permanent settlement, was limited to the land revenue and quit rent (reduced rent) on Inams only. It excluded much to the disadvantage of the Palegar the Moturpha (trade tax) which was to be collected directly by the government through its agencies. One year after the Decennial settlement was fixed, the hopes of the Palegar were raised when in 1815, the Board of Revenue conveyed to the Collector that a Permanent Sanad, as the Palegar has been assiduously asking for, would be soon granted and that the Palegar would be designated as Zamindar. The Collector also conveyed the same to Sankar Royal, the Palegar in October, 1815.[51]

However the hopes of the Zamindar were frustrated when the Court of Directors refused to grant a Permanent Sanad to Punganur chief in 1815, on the ground that the remuneration for the Zamindar under the Decennial Settlement was fixed at a higher rate. The ten year lease thus was to continue till its end. The Court of Directors stated:

> We see no reason however for making an exception in favor of this Poliem (Punganur) from the general instructions which have been conveyed to you (BOR) prohibiting the Permanent Settlement of Districts where that arrangement

has not been already introduced. The settlement therefore be considered limited to the period of Decennial Lease.[52]

When the Decennial Lease was about to end, the Zamindar Sankar Royal wrote to the Governor through the Board of Revenue in 1823 that he be granted Permanent Sanad and given the right to issue pattas to the ryots. The government issued orders authorizing the Zamindar to issue pattas in his own name. Further, the Zamindar was entrusted with the management of the Zamindari under the general supervision of the District Collector. By allowing the Zamindar to issue pattas, the government loosened one more link in the chain of its control. But the Permanent Sanad was no where in sight.

In March 1830, on the death of Sankar Royal, the Zamindar, his son Immadi Chikka Royal succeeded to the Zamindari. The Collector while writing to the Board on the affairs of the Zamindari, suggested that the Permanent Settlement be made with the new Zamindar. To drive his point, the Collector pointed out as to how the suspense with the temporary leases in Punganur were telling on the economic well being of the very people there. He pointed out that the "Zamindar was burdened with debts, and if temporary leases were to continue, the welfare of the people was sure to be affected".[53]

The government while recognizing the succession of Nana Sahib as the new Zamindar, conferred the management of the Zamindari, "on the same terms as those on which his father had held"[54]. On 10 May, 1831 the Zamindar was formally invested by the Collector on behalf of the Governor with the presentation of *Killuut* and Dress of Honor, a practice generally adopted only in the case of permanently settled Zamindaries. Because of this honor, Punganur continued to be called 'Zamindari' and the chief, 'Zamindar' though the issue of granting of a permanent Sanad was delayed till 1861. However, the government decided that pending a reference to the application of the Zamindar to the Board of Revenue, Punganur Zamindari was given to the Zamindar on an annual peishcush of Rs. 63,000 rupees and excluding him of submitting his accounts to the Collector.[55] Freeing the Zamindar from submitting annual accounts though was a major relief, yet the much awaited permanent settlement alluded Punganur leading to the uncertainty in matters of revenue collections.

Peishcush on Progressive scale (1833-1852)

In Punganur, because of the failure of seasons and the inability of the ryots in paying land rents, there was a time when the peishcush, the annual amount to be paid by the Zamindar, was fixed on a progressive scale giving concession due to the prevailing drought conditions. The Zamindar, Immadi Pedda Chikka Royal, in a petition to the government in 1830 urged the reduction in the peishcush amount of Rs. 63,000, that was fixed in 1815. But due to the general remissions given to the ryots to the tune of 1/3 and ¼ on wet and dry lands respectively, by the government, there was considerable reduction in the total revenues collected and the Zamindar was at a great disadvantage due to such a reduction in the revenues.

The Collector of Cuddapah, James Dalzell in his report sent on 5 January, 1831 reiterated that the Zamindar was in a disadvantageous position as the Inams were taken away, the reduction in rents were effected on the ryots and that the Moturpha, Sayer and Abkari taxes were also taken off from the purview of the Zamindar. In view of the changed situation, the Collector cautioned that there was every likelihood in the Zamindari that "it would have the effect of driving ryots into the neighboring Taluks as well as into North Arcot and even to Mysore".[56] Further he suggested that the Zamindar be handed over the 215 Inam Villages taken by the government earlier.

The government having concurred with the opinion of the Collector, felt the peishcush amount Rs. 63,000 on the Zamindar to be heavy. To show consideration to the Zamindar, the government wanted to fix the amount at a lower rate and increase it gradually on a progressive scale over a period of years. The Board of Revenue directed the Collector to work out the details and report "at what rate and within what period" the assessment of Punganur be raised to the usual rate. [57] The Collector, H. Lacon, after examining the cultivation accounts of the Zamindari of the earlier leases, wrote to the government as to how the unfavorable seasons of the previous years have badly affected agriculture in Punganur.

The report of the Collector convinced the Board of Revenue on the immediate need of fixing the peishcush at a lower rate to benefit the Zamindar without causing much loss to the government. The Board suggested to the government the details of the arrangement thus:

> The annual peishcush on Punganur shall be Rs. 51,000 for three years from 1833, that it shall be raised to Rs. 52,000 in the fourth and a similar addition of 1000 rupees shall subsequently be made to it every alternate year until it reached the amount of Rs. 57,000 in the fourteenth and thereafter every year there shall be a uniform increase of Rs.1,000 until the twentieth year when it will have Rs. 63,000.[58]

The progressive scale thus fixed in 1833 reached its maximum after twenty years in 1852. The government decided to settle Punganur revenues for the next five years on the usual peishcush of Rs. 63,000 a year, disregarding the pleas of the Zamindar for a permanent Sanad. During this period, the Zamindar Mummadi Pedda Chikka Royal died (1843) and his son Sankar Royal II succeeded as the Zamindar. While the five year lease was in force, Punganur was transferred in 1856 from the jurisdiction of Cuddapah district to North Arcot with its headquarters at Chittoor.[59]

On the completion of the Five Year lease in 1858, the Collector of North Arcot district, P. Wittingham wrote to the Board of Revenue pleading for Permanent Sanad to be granted to Punganur on the ground that the temporary leases would not provide any inducement to improve the Zamindari. If it was not possible, the Collector suggested that at least a perpetual lease for Rs. 63,000 should be granted to the Zamindar.[60] The Zamindar, Sankar Royal II in a petition to the Governor in 1858 recalling how Punganur was kept under periodical leases for a protracted period urged that a permanent Sanad be granted to him. [61]

The Board of Revenue at last decided to recommend to the government to grant Permanent Sanad to Punganur. It also wrote to the government that Sankar Royal was a competent person and that the interests of the people of the Zamindari would be safe in his hands. The government also in the meantime felt that it was not expedient and wise to cancel the Zamindars and introduce Ryotwari and thus reduce all parts of the country to a dumb uniformity. The change in the policy of the government was also due to the shift of its disposition towards the Indian aristocracy after the outbreak of the 1857 Revolt and the subsequent Queen's proclamation, next year. It obviously wanted to maintain the landed gentry as a social buttress and as a general policy of sanctioning Permanent Settlement of land revenue on such estates hitherto kept on temporary leases.[62]

Permanent Sanad (1861)

After keeping Punganur in temporary leases for more than sixty years from 1802, the Government of Madras sought the approval of the Secretary of State for India, to grant Permanent Sanad to Punganur. Sir Charles Wood, the Secretary of State in a prompt dispatch to the Governor of Madras in approval, wrote "to grant unto Raja Sugutur Immadi Sankar Royalu Yashovanta Bahadur and his heirs a permanent title to the Punganur estate subject to the payment of an annual peishcush of Rs. 63,000".[63] The Government of Madras then directed the Board to prepare a Sanad to be given to the Zamindar and also inform him accordingly.

The Zamindar, Sankar Royal was thus finally granted the Sanad on 1 February, 1861[64]. Though some of his long standing demands were not met by the government, the Zamindar felt gratified over the granting of the Permanent Settlement as the suspense over the absence of it was finally over. The Sanad was in force till the very abolition of the Zamindaries after India became free by implementing the "Abolition of Zamindaries and Conversion to Ryotwari Act" in 1948 by the Congress government in Madras.

The numerous revenue settlements the British made during the period from 1802 when Punganur came under their indirect control till 1861 when finally Permanent Settlement was made, reflect their general policy of deriving more income with less expenditure. At the start itself, the punitive peishcush of 20,000 pagodas imposed by Tipu Sultan of Mysore was retained by the British as it suited them. Thomas Munro on his part, retained the high peishcush, but got the survey and settlement done as in the Ryotwari tenures. Punganur, because of its significant role played from the pre-colonial times, was the only Palem in the entire Ceded Districts to be retained under the Zamindar. However, during the period of temporary leases, there was great uncertainty on the continuity of the Zamindari and this naturally affected the economic situation of the Zamindari. The higher peishcush imposed on the Zamindar not only affected the finances, but also cast a heavy tax burden on the peasantry and thus became a potential cause for the recurring famines and scarcities in the Zamindari during the entire 19th. Century.

Notes

1. The word *Teerva* is derived from the Telugu word, *Theerpu*, which means settled or fixed of money valuation. See for details, Settlement Report of George Straton, 14 July 1801, quoted in *Proceedings of BOR,* 11 December, 1869, No. 9078, p. 9632.
2. Theoretically, *Patta* was the title deed which ensured the right of the peasant to hold the land. Dharma Kumar, however has argued how the patta itself was not the title deed in the strict sense of the term because of the inaccuracies in their entries" See for details, Dharma Kumar, 'Land Ownership and Inequality in Madras Presidency, 1853-54 to 1946-47.' In The Indian Economic and Social History Review, (IESHR) Vol. XII, No. 3, July –September, 1975, p. 231.
3. Soils having the same grain out-turn are placed on Tharam or grade. The main object of classification under Tharam was to make it more clear to the ryots. See, History of Land Revenue Settlements, (Madras, 1976) P. 7. The present writer is informed by the elderly villagers that they heard from their forefathers that Thomas Munro, the Collector used to put a pinch of earth in his mouth and decided the Tharam or grade of that land based on the salt the land contained. Munro thus was a walking laboratory to test the quality of lands. This interesting information however is not recorded by Munro anywhere in his reports.
4. *Report on the Administration of Madras Presidency, During the Year, 1872-73*, (Madras, 1874)p. 15.
5. In the case of Northern Circars, the Zamindars collected rent in kind till the Estate Land Act 1908 came into force. For details, see, A. Satyanarayana, "Commutation of rent in Andhra Estates, 1908-1934,", paper presented at the Indian History Congress, 39th. Session, Hyderabad, December, 28-30, 1978.
6. B. Danam, "Chittoor District Plan 1974", (un published Report), Collector's Record Office, Chittoor District, p. 16.

7. E. Krishnamurthy, "Thettupalle", in Gilbert Slater, (Ed),*Some South Indian Villages*, (London, 1918) p. 97.
8. Dietmar Rothermund, "Government, Land Lord and Tenant", *Indian Economic and Social History Review,* Vol. VI, No. 4, December, 1969, Pp. 351-352.
9. Dharma Kumar, Land and Cast in South India, : Agriculture Labour in the Madras Presidency During the Nineteenth Century, (Cambridge, 1965), p. 29.
10. S. Sundar Raja Iyengar, *Land Tenures in Madras Presidency,* Pp. 113-119
11. R.E. Frykenberg has divided all the Inams in to 4 divisions. i.e. Socio-religious; socio-political; Social service and socio-economic. For details see his, "Silent Settlements in South India, 1793-1853", in Frykenberg (Ed), *Land Tenure and Peasant in South Asia,* New Delhi, 1977, p. 50.
12. Eric Stokes, "Privileged Land Tenure in Village India, in Early 19th. Century," in R.E. Frykenberg (Ed), *Land Tenure and Peasant in South Asia,*New Delhi, 1977, p. 56.
13. Amaram was a grant of land by the Zamindar or Palegar on condition of service; and it was resumable on the failure of such a service. See, W.T. Blair to R.A. Dalzell, 30 October, 1869, Inam Papers, Appendix-B.
14. S. Sundar Raja Iyengar, *Land Tenures in Madras Presidency,* Pp. 138-141.
15. Robert Ross, Collector of Cuddapah to the Board of Revenue, No. 111, 26 August, 1811, Cuddapah District Records (CDR), State Archives, Hyderabad, Vol. 653, p. 289.
16. S. Sundar Raja Iyengar, Op.cit, p. 120.
17. Robert Ross, Collector of Cuddapah to the Board of Revenue, (BOR), In General Reports of the BOR, 1815, p. 66.
18. Memoranda from Immadi Chikka Royal to Mr. Dalzell, Collector of Cuddapah, appended in Collector's letter o D. Elliot, Secretary, BOR, in C.D.R. Vol. 4579, p. 521.
19. Letter from J.D. Robinson, Collector of North Arcot District, to the Inspector of Police, 24 August, 1867, No, 136, Proceedings of the BOR, no. 4029, 5 June, 1869, p. 4429.

20. Robert Ross to BOR, 22 November, 1813, State Archives, Hyderabad C.D.R, No. 331, Vol. 655, p. 246.
21. Walter Kelley Firminger,(Ed), *Historical Introduction to the Bengal Portion of Fifth Report,* rpt. (New Delhi), p. 324.
22. General Reports of the Board of Revenue to the Hon. Governor in Council, sent to the Court of Directors, from 26 Dec, 1815 to 6 January, 1817, Vol. 21 to 23 (Madras, 1876) p. 72.

23,24,25. Settlement Reports of the Ceded Districts for 1802-03, from Thomas Munro to the President and members of the BOR, see, C.D.R. Vol. 647.

26. General Reports of the BOR Op.cit, p. 72.
27. Report of the Committee of the House of Commons on the Corn Laws, ordered to be printed,26 July 1814, General Reports of the Board of Revenue, CDR, *Ibid*, p. 73.
28. *Ibid,* p. 74.
29. Memorial from Sankar Royal II, Zamindar of Punganur to Sir Frederick Temple and Karl Dufferin, Governor-General of India, January 1885, para,13. This memorial (Arzi) was sent with a request for a permanent reduction of Rs. 21,000 from the peishcush amount in view of the reduction of assessment rates in 1824.
30. Text of Memorandum by the Zamindar of Punganur, 6 January, 1938 see Estate Land Act Committee Report (Prakasam Committee Report) Part IV, (Madras 1938), p. 180.
31. S. Sundar Raja Iyengar, Land Tenures in Madras Presidency, (Madras, 1933), p. 197.
32. Privy Council Judgment quoted in History of Land Revenue Settlement and abolition of Intermediary Tenures in Tamil Nadu, (Madras, 1976), p. 77.
33. For a detailed discussion on the causes that led to the introduction of the Permanent System of land Revenue also known as Zamindari system or Cornwallis system, see, Richard Temple, *Men and Events of My Time in India,* p. 30, quoted, Edward Thompson and G.T. Garratt, *Rise and Fulfillment of British Rule in India*, rpt. Allahabad, 1976, p. 191.
34. Letter from Lord Cornwallis to the Court of Directors, 2 May, 1792, in W.F. Firminger,(Ed), The Fifth Report of Select

Committee, for the Affairs of the East India Company, 28 July, 1812, (Calcutta, 1918), Vol. II, p. 250.

35,36. The Sanad was issued in the name of Immadi Shankar Royal, the then Zamindar of Punganur, on 1 February, 1861. The Sanad document contains the names of all the villages appended to the Zamindari.

37. Punganur was transferred in parts to the Ceded Districts from Baramahal in 1802 and from Mysore in 1803. It is to be noted that about eighty such Palegars in the Ceded districts were dispossessed by Thomas Munro. See "Memorandum of the Poligars of the Ceded Districts", enclosed in the Report of the Principal Collector of the Ceded Districts, dated, 20 March, 1802, in F.W. Firminger, Fifth Report, Vol. II, Appendix, 26. pp. 429-530

38. Letter from Thomas Munro to William Petrice, President, BOR, 8 March, 1802, in Cuddapah District Records (CDR), Vol. 647, p. 285. Andhra Pradesh State Archives, Hyderabad

39. A Controy Pagoda was equal to Rs. 3.

40. Rent Collection Report of the Ceded Districts submitted by Thomas Munro to the Board of Revenue, 2 May, 1803, C D R Vol. 648, Para 18, p. 306.

41. A note in Munro's Diary states; June 28, 1807 – Ordered the Surveyors in Punganoor to come to Anantapur, (Headquarter for the Collector then), whenever the measurement is finalized in order to be paid off". C D R. Vol. 5161, 28 June, 1807.

42. *Ibid*, 30 January, 1806 to 27 February, 1807.

43. Memorial submitted by Raja Sankar Royal, to Chaplin, the Collector, 29 June, 1808, Aminigunta Sankar Royal Collections (ASR collections), Vol. 2, Doc. 16 a, p. 5.

44. Letter from the Collector, W. H. Chaplain, to the President and Members of the Board of Revenue, 5, December, 1808, CDR, Vol. 662, Para, 283, p. 242.

45. Letter from W. Wyne, the Secretary, BOR, to Chaplin, the Collector of the Ceded Districts, 16 December, 1808, ASR collections, Vol. 2, p. 1.

46. *Ibid,* Para, 4.

47. The Triennial settlement was beset with several drawbacks. In 1823, Smalley the Collector of Nellore wrote in his settlement Report

about this form of settlement: "Lands changed, ryots ousted, accounts neglected, industry checked, manyams usurped, tanks allowed to go ruin, cultivation carried on slovenly", see C. *Rundall, Settlement Report of Nellore, 1870.*

48. Abstract of Ross Statement of Report to the BOR, 26 August, 1811, CDR, Vol. 665, p. 476.
49. Letter from Robert Ross, the Collector of Ceded Districts to the BOR, dated, 22 September, 1811, CDR, vol. 653, p. 353.
50. *Ibid.*
51. Letter from Robert Ross, the Collector to the BOR, 22 November, 1813, CDR, Vol. 655.

52,53. Extracts from the Parwana Books, Taluk Punganoor, For Fasli, 1223, 11 June, 1814, A S R Collections, Vol. 2, Doc. 17, p. 1.

54. Letter from the Collector of Cuddapah, to Sankar Royal, is quoted by his uncle Mummadi Chikka Royal to the Collector of Cuddapah, 5 November, 1815, see, A.S.R. Collections, Vol. 2, Doc. 19, A.

55,56. General letter from the Court of Directors to Board of Revenue, Madras, 22 May, 1818, para, 82 see BOR Proceedings, 14 January, 1863, p. 200.

57. Letter from the Collector of Cuddapah (Camp Madanapalle) 30 March, 1830, ASR Collections, vol. 2, Doc. 36, p. 1.
58. H. Chamier, Secretary to Government (Revenue Department) No. 516, 4 June, 1830, ASR Collections Vol. 2, Doc, 39.
59. Canning, Secretary to Government, addressed to the BOR, 7 June, 1831, no. 10, *ASR Collections,* Vol. 2, Doc. 44.
60. Letter from J.A. Dalzell to James Lushington, Secretary to Government, 5 January, 1831, CDR Vol. 4579 para. 5, p. 533.
61. D. Elliot, Secretary to BOR, to the Principal Collector of Cuddapah, 30 May, 1831, ASR Collections, Vol. 2, D. 43, p. 1.
62. Letter from J.C. Morris, Acting Secretary to the BOR, to the Chief Secretary to Government, (Revenue Department), 29 December, 1831, ASR Collections, Vol. 2, Doc. 46.
63. G.O. quoted in the Proceedings of the BOR, No.141 25 May, 1853, ASR Collections Vol. 2, Doc. 82.
64. Letter from P. Wittingham, Collector, N.A. District to J.D. Sim, Secretary, BOR, 25 August, 1858, no. 169.

65. Memorial from Raja Sugutoor Immadi Sankar Royal of Punganur to the Governor-in-Council, Madras, 22 October, 1858. ASR Collections, Vol. 2, Doc. 84.
66. S. Bhattacharya, *Financial Foundations of the British Raj, 1858-1872,* Shimla, 1971, p. 153.
67. Dispatch from Sir Charles Wood, the Secretary of State for India, to the Governor –in – Council, Fort St. George, India Office, London, 20 February, 1860, No.14, India Office Library, London, See for the text of the dispatch, Appendix of this volume.
68. W. Huddleston, Secretary to BOR, to J.D. Bourdillon, Secretary to Government (Revenue Department), 29 January, 1861, No. 511, ASR Collections, Vol., Doc. 87. Also see, G.O. (Revenue Department) 1 February, 1861. No. 263. For the full text of the Sanad, see the Appendix of this volume.

IV

Agricultural Practices

Agriculture constituted the main occupation of the people of the Punganur Zamindari. Caste, with its strong roots in society played an important role in the professions people pursued. While agriculture happened to be the occupation of few upper castes like the Kapu, Reddi and Kamma, professional trades and services were carried on by numerous other castes. The presence of a large number of tribals is a distinguishing feature of the rural scene of Punganur Zamindari. Agriculture remained in a state of stagnation and decay in the Zamindari particularly in the 19th Century. Punganur had been an area of small holdings with low density of population. Vast stretches of uncultivated lands were a common feature of this Zamindari. As agriculture became quite often an uneconomic enterprise, many ryots used to take up rearing of cattle by making use of the pastures found in the fringes of jungles. Desertion of land and migrations were also not infrequent. The adherence of the ryots to conventional crop patterns and implements, and their aversion to take to any modern commercial crops also affected the agrarian growth of the Zamindari. The crop patterns and the agricultural practices in the Zamindari over the 19th and early 20th Centuries reveal only a snap- shot picture of the state of economy with little or no prospect of change for the better.

Demographic Features

Punganur recorded a steady increase in its population ranging from two to twenty percent during every decade in the 19th century except for the twenty percent reduction as per the census of 1881, due to the unprecedented starvation deaths during the Great Famine of 1876. Between 1871, when the first census enumeration was taken, and 1981 there had been a hundred percent rise in the population. The following table shows the rate of growth of population in the Zamindari.

Table 4-1

Year	*Population*	*Decade's Variation*	*Per centage of variation*
1871	1,09,282	——	——
1881	88,426	- 21,856	- 20.0
1891	91,852	+ 3,426	+ 3.38
1901	96,852	+ 5,000	+ 5.45
1911	1,07,051	+ 10,199	+10.53
1921	1,09,391	+ 2,340	+2.19
1931	1,22,271	+ 12,880	+11,77
1941	1,34,487	+12,216	+ 9.99
1951	1,47,398	+ 12,911	+ 9.60
1961	1,68,850	+21,452	+ 14.55
1971	2,01,596	+ 32,746	+ 19.41
1981	2,41,718	+ 40,122	+ 20.01

Source: District Census Handbooks of the relevant periods and also M. Somasekhara Sarma (Ed.) *Vignana Sarvaswamu* (Telugu Bhasha Samithi, Madras, 1961) p. 1336.

As far as the density of population, Punganur had the lowest for the entire District. As per the 1871 census, Punganur had 168 persons per square mile. Even after a period of five decades, it stood as the lowest in the district as 169 persons in 1921.[1] In 1931 it rose to 189; in 1961 it stood at 254 and in 1971 it rose to 311 persons.[2] As regards the social composition, the majority of the people were Hindus, with the hierarchy of their caste system. While Brahmins, Reddies, Kammas and Balijas belonged to the land owning upper castes, professional artisans and craftsmen composed of castes, belonged to the second category. Landless agricultural labor and those who worked on leather, came in the last category. There were also several tribals like Sugalis, Yanadis and Irulas. The Sugalis also known as *Lambadis* for, they spoke a dialect *Lambadi* and their settlements were called *Thandas*. Each of such settlement had a headman after whom the *Thanda* was known.[3]

The Muslims constituted a small percentage of the total population of the Zamindari. While in 1871 they accounted for 3.78 percent with a total 4,049, in 1921 the percentage rose to 7.88 with a total of 8,031 persons[4]. Most of the Muslims were engaged in agriculture, working as laborers. There were also among them artisans like carpenters, Blacksmiths and knife sharpeners. A separate category among Muslim converts, *Dudekulas* who practiced many Hindu customs, were engaged in cotton cleaning and bed- stitching.[5] The Christians constituted yet another segment in the society. Though Christian population was numerically less even today, Christianity came to Punganur very early. The earliest conversion for the whole of the Telugu speaking area in the erstwhile Madras Presidency, took place in Punganur in 1701 when Fr. Medwit, a French missionary baptized a widow and her children. By 1735, a Roman Catholic Church was also built here.[6] With the establishment of the American Arcot Mission (AAM), in 1851, Protestant Mission activities started in Punganur. Dr. Jacob Chamberlain, an American Missionary established himself in Madanapalle in 1863 and with him began active missionary efforts in this region which was known as ' Village Movement'. He often visited Punganur and even had cordial relations with the Zamindar, Shankar Royal II.[7] In 1871, the total Christian population in Punganur was 187, in 1921 it rose to 326 and by 1931 it was 463.[8]

Land Utilization

The cultivation statistics about Punganur Zamindari from the beginning of the 19th Century, are found in the statements sent by the Principal Collector, Thomas Munro to the Board of Revenue. All the cultivable land in the Zamindari was divided into Dry (Punja) and Wet(Nanja) categories. From 1804-05, another category called, 'garden lands' was added. The cultivation accounts for Punganur during the period of Thomas Munro's Collectorship (1800-1807) were as follows:

Table 4-2

Year	*Dry lands in acres*	*Garden lands in acres*	*Wet lands in acres*
1800-01	22,215	—	5,035
1801-02	20,218	—	4,854
1802-03	37,057	—	4,947
1803-04	42,853	—	5,419
1804-05	42,999	451	5,311
1805-06	42,755	422	7,255
1806-07	19,493	124	2,084

Source: Report for the Ceded Districts from Fasli 1210 to 1226 sent to Board of Revenue by Thomas Munro, 15 August 1807, in Ferminger (Ed.), *Fifth Report*, Vol. II, pp. 662-663.

The total extent of land under cultivation, interestingly enough, did not vary much during the entire 19th Century. In 1881, it was estimated that dry land under cultivation was 32,000 acres, wet land 9,000 acres and garden lands 4,000 acres.[9] By 1930 the total extent of agricultural land in the Zamindari was

5,23,393 acres. Of this, Inam lands covered 88,453 acres and the Zamindari lands 4,34,940 acres.[10] The proportion of the total cultivated land in Punganur had always been much lower than the total surveyed land. This anomaly was due to the absence of any permanent large-scale irrigation works. The total cultivable lands in the Zamindari comprised of cultivable wastes, current fallows and the net-cropped area which came to an extent of 1,64,743 acres and thus accounted to 31.44 percent of the total 5,23,393 acres in the entire Zamindari.[11]

Irrigation

In Punganur, the prospect of cultivation of lands depended entirely on the monsoon The average rainfall for Punganur for the period 1873 to 1930, was mere 28.11 inches. The distribution of the average rainfall during the above period was as follows:

Table 4-4

Months	*Average rainfall in inches (1873- 1930)*
January	0.40
February	0.31
March	0.39
April	1.00
May	2.60
June	1.93
July	2.81
August	3.65
September	5.21
October	5.05
November	3.96
December	0.86
The whole year	28.11

Source: Statistical Appendix for Chittoor District, (Madras, 1932), Vol. III, p. 34.

The average rainfall in the Zamindari was much less than other Zamindaries in the District. For example, Kalahasthi for the period from 1877 to 1930 recorded an annual rainfall of 43.40 inches and in Karvetinagar for the same period it was 39.01 inches.[12]

Thus with rainfall very scanty, the only irrigation sources in the Zamindari were tanks and wells. Punganur had the largest number of tanks for the entire District. There were altogether 1,374 tanks and 1,147 wells in the Zamindari.[13] Owing to the hilly nature of the area, numerous tanks were formed to retain rain water. As the tanks were constructed in chain down the different valleys, the breaching of the top one generally resulted in the breach of all the lower ones whenever there were heavy rains.[14] As most of the tanks in the Zamindari were small, like puddles, ryots dug wells wherever they found feasible. Crops like sugarcane depended mainly on well water as the water in tanks would not last round the year. The *Kapila,* with a huge leather bucket drawn by a pack of bullock was the only common mode for lifting water. The ryots were averse to adopt any other mode to lift the water because of the high costs involved in any improved methods.[15]

The total irrigated lands in the Zamindari and the sources of irrigation were as follows:

Table 4-5

Sources		*Area irrigated in acres*
By private canals		14
By tanks		24,644
By wells		455
	Total:	25,113

Source: Statistical Appendix for Chittoor Dist. (Madras, 1932) Vol. III, p. 15.

When the total cultivable land which included the cultivable wastes, current fallows and the net cropped area was taken into account, the total irrigated area in the Zamindari accounted for mere 15 percent. But of the net cropped area of 65,028 acres, the irrigated lands accounted for 38 percent. The remaining 62 percent came under dry lands.[16]

Livestock

As returns through agriculture were marginal, the ryots in Punganur were made to look for rearing of the livestock . Cattle played a crucial role for cultivation and for transport. The vast forests in the Zamindari provided the needed extensive pasture lands. Punganur had been famous for a special breed of cattle known as "Punganur breed" like the Ongole breed in Nellore, the Kangayams in Coimbatore, the Knangoondis in Kuppam and Hallikars in Mysore.[17]

The Punganur bunga now almost an endangered species is most sought after due to its high-fat milk yield, low weight and small size. The Punganur cow measures around 60 to 80cm in height and weighs less than 50 Kilos. Thus it is considered as the world's shortest breed of cows. Even the Dexter Cow of the United Kingdom that holds the Guinness book of world records at present, measures 85 cm. There is an attempt by the biodiversity department, Andhra Pradesh, to get the geographical indicator (GI) tag for the Punganur dwarf cow.

Lauding the quality of the Punganur breed, particularly of the cows, the Collector, Whiteside wrote thus in 1880:

> The quality of milk cows of this breed gave was comparatively small, but was of very good quality. The Punganur cows were usually of small size, short in barrel, thin legs and tail, and generally dappled dark brown and white. Since my return to the District in 1871 as Collector, I cannot call to

mind having seen a single cow of pure Punganur breed. The Zamindar who owns a large number of cows has not one of that breed.[18]

The cattle fairs held annually in Punganur attracted the villagers from far and near to buy and sell their cattle in such annual fairs. Weekly shandies also were the venues for such cattle transactions. Certain hair-marks on the cattle supposed to bring luck to the buyer influenced the prices of the cattle.

Avulapalle, which means the village of cows, was a major center for Punganur cattle because of its proximity to the vast pastures as the place happens to be near the thick jungles. Palamanda, which means a herd of milking cows was another center of Punganur cattle. The quality of Punganur breed as the Collector Whiteside had reported, deteriorated by the end of the century. The deterioration of cattle wealth in general and the Punganur breed in particular, could be ascribed to the decline in the extent and quality of the grazing lands and also to the destruction of the forests for timber, firewood and coal.[19] On the suggestion of the Department of Agriculture, the Government of Madras in 1881 directed that necessary steps should be initiated to improve the breed.

The fat content in the milk of the Punganur Bunga is said to be 8 to 10 percent and thus almost equal to that of the buffalo milk while the normal cow's milk usually has a fat content not exceeding 3 or 3.5 percent. Besides, the Punganur Dwarf cow's milk is also reported to contain religious and sentimental significance. Suvignanam Ashram in the outskirts of Hyderabad on the Medak highway in its large farm of cows, also has few Punganur breed of cows. On the numerous advantages of this breed, the chief of the Ashram, Swami Sathyavir says: "We have got the pure breed of the Punganur dwarf cow variety from the government livestock farm at Palamaner in Chittoor District.

This cow needs only a small space, and can survive epidemic outbursts easily and its water and fodder consumption is minimal". The cow is also known to have high levels of immunity, is drought resistant and its milk and ghee is reported to have medicinal properties. Though the breed, in its purest form is almost extinct, it is still rated as one of the major breeds in the region. It is interesting to note that the Sri Venkateswara University of Veterinary Sciences, Tirupati, as recently as in 2007, initiated a project to take necessary steps to revive the Punganur breed of cows.

Punganur also has been known for the breed of small, black faced wooly sheep. This breed was especially favored for its thick growth of wool. Ramasamudram area of the Zamindari has been famous for weaving the coarse *cumblies* (rugs) with the sheep wool. With a view to encourage cattle rearing, successive Collectors of the District introduced a special breed of sheep and also new varieties of grass that cattle liked most. In 1871 the Collector, Whiteside, issued a circular to the Thahsildar to find out from the local shepherds as the types of grass the cattle of the locality liked most so that such grass could be grown on hill-slopes and tank beds. He even suggested to the Commissioner of land settlement that some seeds of the famous 'Salt bush' should be imported from Australia as that fodder, which according to him, had the "marvelous capacity for withstanding drought." Similarly he tried to introduce a special breed of sheep from the government Agricultural farm in Saidapet, Madras. But these experiments were not successful as the local people generally preferred the local breeds.

The cattle were frequently affected by a variety of diseases like the Rinderpest, Foot and mouth diseases etc. Locally these diseases were known as *Kumara, Domma, Musara* etc,.[20] In the absence of veterinary medical care, the ryots followed conventional local remedies made of oils, spices and herbs. It was not until the Institute of Veterinary Preventive Medicine was established in 1932 in Madras that the anti-Rinderpest serum was produced and vaccination against such diseases came into vogue. Whenever cattle diseases broke out, the District Collector prohibited the cattle fairs and cattle shandies by invoking the Madras Cattle Diseases Act of 1866. This was as a precautionary measure to contain the diseases.

Implements

The agricultural operations in the Zamindari were carried on with traditional, locally made implements. There were three different ploughs which were in use. The smallest one was for irrigated lands, the larger one for dry lands and the largest one for occasional use in the sandy and loamy soils. Other popularly used implements were, *Gorru,* the bamboo drill, *Palakiguntaka*, for pulverizing the soil, *Palikimanu*, to cover the soil after sowing etc. The other smaller implements were *Mamoti* or *Para,* crowbar, sickle, short handled hoe etc. Drilling in seed was widely practiced.[21] The ryots generally preferred the indigenous implements as they were inexpensive, light, portable, easy to make or repair with locally available materials. The government's efforts, as in the case of cattle rearing, to introduce newly developed, labour efficient instruments like the 'Climax Plough', did not bear any fruit.

Crops

There were three main cropping seasons in Punganur Zamindari. *Kharif* season from June to December, late *Kharif* season from September to March and *Rabi* season from December to April. The main Kharif and Rabi crops were locally known as Samba and *Vaisakham* respectively. The late Kharif or mid season is known as *Kar*. The Kharif is the most important one as wet and dry crops were cultivated during that period.

A perusal of cultivation accounts of the Zamindari of 1932 shows that out of the total area cropped (that includes *fasaljasthi* or the second crop) 88 percent was under food crops like Rice, Cumbu and Ragi; four percent was under oil seeds like Gingelly (sesame seeds), Groundnut and Castor; and eight percent under commercial crops such as Sugar cane, Spices, Tobacco, fodder, orchards and other non-food crops.[21]

The wet lands, known as Nanja, yielded generally two crops, while the dry lands known as Punja yielded only one crop a year. In Punganur, there were no lands which yielded three crops a year as there was always paucity for water. Cattle dung and farm yard wastes were generally used as manure. The green manure was taken on contract from the forests belonging to the Zamindar. *Pungamia glabra* trees were specially grown by ryots for the sake of green manure. Tank-soil was also extensively used as manure particularly for dry lands. Folding of sheep during nights on open fields on ploughed soil was widely practiced. This type of manuring was considered good for certain crops like Chillies. The awareness of the importance of manuring is revealed through a number of proverbs prevalent in this region. "If the land is manured, even a mad person can cultivate", is one such proverb commonly heard in Punganur.

The methods of cultivation of few crops like Paddy, Ragi, Sugarcane, Groundnut etc. deserve special mention. Paddy was raised under wells and tanks and the area under Paddy cultivation amounted to 30 percent of the total cultivated area. The popular strains of Paddy were, *Jilakara Samba, Chinna Samba* and *Pulla Samba*. Finer varieties of Paddy took four to six months to mature while the inferior varieties took much less.

The paddy growing season generally went with the monsoons. For the first crop, the seed is sown in June or July and harvested in December, for the second crop the seed was sown in December or January and harvested in April or May.

Paddy was sown only on three days in the week as people here believed they were auspicious. The local priest is also consulted for the selection of the day to sow seeds. Another practice in this region was that shortly before harvest of Paddy, ryots of the village would join together, slaughter a sheep, mix its blood with rice and scatter it over the crop in the belief that it would give more yield.

New strains of Paddy that matured at a quicker pace became popular only after the establishment of the Paddy breeding station at Coimbatore in 1913, followed by a chain of sub-stations in the entire Madras Presidency.

Paddy crop was generally affected by a number of pests. The most common in Punganur were *Paddy Blight* (Tella Cheeda), *Helminto Sporium Blight* (Pedda Cheeda) and *Foot rot* (Kondapi Rogam). The ryots believed that plant diseases were the visitations of malevolent spirits. Sheep or pigs or white fowls were offered to propitiate such spirits. The spread of pests to a large extent was checked by the insectivorous birds and few types of eagles which were also de-notified by the government as "Protected Birds". The cultivation of Ragi as a second crop on irrigated lands was confined to the areas with assured water supply. Because of the cool climate that the area enjoyed compared to the neighboring Taluks, Ragi was also sown broadcast on dry lands. Ragi happens to be the staple food of the village poor, while consumption of rice was usually confined to richer classes.

Sugarcane and Groundnut occupied the primary place among the commercial crops in the Zamindari. As sugarcane crop takes nearly a year to mature, its cultivation was confined to areas with assured water supply. Though there was general decline in the cultivation of Sugarcane by 1879 due to stoppage of local distillation of spirit from molasses, by 1942 its cultivation showed a steady progress throughout the District.[22]

Groundnut was sown in the dry lands of the Zamindari. Though the cultivation of groundnut was known earlier, it was only at the turn of the 20th Century, that the weather resistant improved varieties of groundnut seed were imported from abroad and made popular in the entire Presidency. On the suggestion of the Madras Chamber of Commerce, the government imported few bags of superior varieties of seed from countries like Senegal, Mozambique, Japan and America, got them sown at the Agricultural farm at Saidapet and distributed the produce as seed to the ryots.[23] The introduction of the new seed paved the way for rapid expansion of cultivation as a major commercial crop and the ryots in Punganur immediately took to the improved varieties of groundnut seed.

Dry crops like groundnut and ragi were seldom sown alone in the Zamindari. They were always associated with mixed cropping. The nine kinds of pulses called *Navadanyams* were sown along with the main crops. While *Gogu* (Bombay Hemp) was grown with Sugarcane on wet lands, Castor, Maize, Jowar etc. were sown along with groundnut. It was believed that mixed cropping would help maintain the quality of the soil and also provide millets and pulses for the family use. As the period of harvest was spread over a longer period under mixed cropping, it provided extended employment to the farmer's family.[24] Cotton cultivation was not popular in Punganur. During 1925-26, it is recorded that a mere 19 acres of land was under cotton cultivation.

There were few unsuccessful attempts on the part of the government to introduce money spinning crops like Cocoa and Eucalyptus at the close of the 19th Century. In 1888 the Commissioner of land settlement, attracted by the reports about the experiments conducted by Dr. Bidie on the cultivation of Cocoa in Peru, in South America, wanted to get it popularized in the Madras Presidency. He advised the Agri- Horticultural

Society, Madras, to send 40 plants of *Erithrovian* Cocoa to the Collector of North Arcot District along with written instructions regarding the method of cultivating the plant. The Collector selected Punganur as the ideal place for the experiment and sent the plants to the Zamindar. Accordingly they were planted on 2 March 1889 and the Zamindar optimistically wrote to the Collector that they would all come up well. But unfortunately all the plants withered away. Like Cocoa, Eucalyptus was also tried unsuccessfully in Punganur in the same year.[25] A successful adoption of such cash crops would have transformed the very pattern of the economy of the Zamindari and would have insulated against the numerous scarcities and a series of famines the Zamindari suffered.

The efforts of the Collector to get some exotic commercial crops popularized in Punganur were but an echo of the policies of the British government at Madras. Dharma Kumar has well assessed the attempts of the government in this direction. She wrote:

(The Government)....made many attempts to introduce various commercial crops including the establishment of experimental farm, the grant of advances for cultivation and the rewards for excellence and the distribution of seeds.[26]

While trying to introduce the commercial crops like sugarcane, groundnut, cocoa etc. the government also took steps to eradicate the obnoxious *Pricklypear* plants which abounded all over the Zamindari and thus interfered with cultivation. The discovery of an insect that ate away the plant, made the task easy in exterminating this hazardous plant.

Wages

Regarding the wages for the farm laborers, generally cash payments were made in Punganur Zamindari. In 1865, as in the entire District, a male coolie was paid two annas (12 Naya Paise at the present reckoning) and a female coolie, one anna per day during the cultivating season. By 1917 the wages recorded a marginal rise- men were paid three annas and females two annas a day. If wages were paid in kind, which was in rare cases, three measures of paddy or ragi and a small quantity of food in the afternoon was given for a male coolie. At times male coolie was given two annas and a meal. It may be noted that money wages for agricultural labour even in prosperous regions like the coastal districts did not go up inspite of the increased employment avenues in trade, transport and growth of markets.[27] The unattached agricultural laborers found work in de-husking the tamarind during the lean periods, the wages remaining the same as in agriculture. The wage earning laborers were hard hit during famines as not only cultivation, even de-husking of tamarind came to a halt during scarcities and famines.

The poor soils, frequent failure of monsoon, the absence of any permanent irrigational facilities and the total dependence of the economy on agriculture, have left the Zamindari below the subsistence level. Zamindari economy continued to stagnate with no scope for diversification and was devoid of any dynamism. Except for occasional spurts of normalcy, Punganur remained practically a pocket of poverty.

Notes

1. Statistical Appendix for Chittoor District, (Madras, 1928 and 1932) Vols. II & III.
2. N. Ramesan, (Ed.) *Chittoor District Gazetteer*, (Hyderabad,1979) Annexure-VIII.
3. Edward Thurston, *Castes and tribes of South India,* Vol. VI, K to M, (Madras, 1909) p. 237.
4. A.F. Cox, *A Manual of North Arcot,* p. 230.
5. A representative picture of the caste system that existed in Punganur could be gleaned in A. Chandrasekhar (Ed.)A Monograph on

Palyampalle (Punganur Taluk) (Census of India, 1961) P.1.Also see, E.Krishnamurthy, "Thettupalle", in Gilbert Slater (Ed.) *Economic Studies: Some South Indian Villages,* (London, 1918), p. 102.

6. *Imperial Gazetteer of India,* Provincial series, Madras, Vol. II (Calcutta, 1908) p. 8.
7. Account of the Missions north of the Palar river, furnished by Rev. J. Colgan, Vicar -General of Madras, quoted in A.F. Cox, *A Manual of North Arcot,* p. 407.
8. *Statistical appendix for Chittoor District,* (Madras,) 1928, vol. II, p. 14, & 1932, Vol. III, p. 11.
9. A.F. Cox, *A Manual of North Arcot,* p. 138.
10. *Statistical Appendix for Chittoor District,* Appendix-IV, (Madras, 1932,) Vol. III, p. 15.
11. *Ibid.*
12. Statement of Rainfall in Statistical Appendix for Chittoor Dist (Madras, 1932) Vol. III, pp. 33-34.
13. Proceedings of the Board of Revenue, 2 December, 1891, p. 759.
14. Charles Benson to the BOR, 20 September, 1879, No. 1092, in Proceedings of the BOR, 22 April, 1880, No. 545.
15. W.S. Whiteside, Collector, North Arcot District to the Secretary, BOR, 29 April, 1880 No. 175.
16. Shankar Linge Gowda, *Indian Economic Census,* (Madras, 1936) Vol. III, p. 180.
17. For a detailed description of each of these breeds, see, S.Y. Krishnaswamy, *Rural Problems in Madras,* Monograph, (Madras, 1947) Pp. 188-90.
18. W.S. Whiteside, Collector of North Arcot District to the BOR, 29 April 1880, No. 175, in BOR Proceedings, 27 May, 1880, No. 727, p. 3026.
19. Decline of the forests was a general phenomenon throughout the country. For details see, Gunnar Myrdal, *Asian Drama: An Inquiry into the Poverty of the Nations,* (London, 1968). pp. 438-39.
20. E. Krishnamurthy, 'Thettupalle' in Gilbert Slater Ed., *Some South Indian Villages,* (London, 1918), p. 100.
21. Regarding the origin of the bamboo drill, Charles Benson says that the method was in vogue in India from very ancient days, while in

England according to him, it came to be used only after its invention by Jethro Tull, the father of modern agriculture around 1730. For details see, *Benson Report, Op.Cit.*

21. Shankar Linga Gowda, *Indian Economic Census*, Vol. III, (Madras, 1936), p. 181.
22. A.V. Raman Rao, *Economic Development of Andhra Pradesh,* 1766-1957, (Bombay, 1958) p. 282.
23. Vans Agnew, Chairman, Madras Chamber of Commerce, to the Secretary, Government of Madras in Proceedings of the BOR, 14 February, 1899, No. 58.
24. For a detailed discussion on the feasible advantages of the mixed cropping, refer, Michelle Byrge Mc Alpin, 'Dearth Famine and Risk,' *Journal of Economic History*, Vol. XXXIX, No. 1, March 1979, p. 147.
25. Letter from the Collector, North Arcot District to the BOR, 31 March 1889, in Retained Disposal No. 1532, 7 April 1889.
26. Dharma Kumar, *Land and Caste in South India,* (Cambridge University Press, 1965), p. 113.
27. M. Atchi Reddy, "Official Data on Agricultural wages in the Madras Presidency from 1873", *Indian Economic and Social History Review,* Vol. XIV, No. 4 (October- December 1978), p. 451.

V

Famines During Early Phase: 1800-1860

India, primarily being an agricultural country has been witnessing famines from very early times. There are numerous references to famines in Pali and Sanskrit literature. Even during the Medieval period, famines did occur, but they were few and far between. However, during the British rule, incidence of famines was very frequent, more widespread and oppressively severe. With the advent of the Company administration, there were famines in most parts of the Deccan.

The entire Madras and Bombay Presidencies, besides the native state of Hyderabad along with Berar, and most parts of Orissa that formed part of the Bengal Presidency having almost a common geographical and economic background though contained different language groups were subjected to frequent famines right from the beginning of the 19th Century. Complete dependence on land in the absence of other sources of productive employment, lack of irrigational facilities, drought due to frequent failure of monsoon, lack of proper transport facilities etc. have left the entire Deccan region below the subsistence level. Except for brief spells, Deccan remained virtually a land of poverty and distress during the entire 19th Century.

In 1797 the entire Baramahal, the present Salem District in Madras Presidency experienced a severe famine due to drought. Col. Graham, the District Collector himself had written on the effects of the drought that was then prevailing. Early in 1799, there was scarcity in Gundagal, when the collector was permitted to buy grain on a government account for the purpose of retail sale to the people.[1] Five years later towards the end of 1804, the season was unfavorable and caused severe pressure on the poorer classes in Tanjore and South Arcot Districts. By early 1805, the situation was so acute that the Collector of South Arcot suggested that importation of rice from Bengal should be done by the Government. But the government of Madras expressed its objection to "any interference with the grain market unless it proved absolutely necessary."[2] In the Ceded Districts, the failure of rain in 1803 was followed by a drought of great severity. Thomas Munro, the Principal Collector of the Ceded districts, gave remission to all lands ploughed, but not sown. [3] Punganur Zamindari, on the recommendation of the Principal Collector, was completely transferred to the Madras Presidency by 1802. Munro who often lived in the neighboring Madanapalle, particularly during summer months, due to its salubrious climate as against the torrid weather of Cuddapah, the District headquarters, made frequent visits to Punganur. He had more than once observed the prevalence of famine or near famine conditions in Punganur Zamindari. Robert Ross, the successor of Munro made similar references to the scarcity conditions prevailing in Punganur. While writing to the Board of Revenue in 1811, Ross made it clear that Punganur "suffered during the last two years as more than any of the Sarkar Talooks."[4] In the later part of 1805, a general failure of crops occurred in all parts of the Presidency. The Board of Revenue suggested employment of able-bodied poor on public works. It however objected to the payment in grain as it generally disturbed the market. In 1807 the entire Presidency was again in the grip of drought and scarcity of grain. The mortality figures in the Presidency during the famines of 1805-07 were as follows:

Table No. 5-1

Years	*Deaths*
1805	3,225
1806	4,902
1807	17,207

Source: Dalzell, *The Madras Famine of 1866*, Para 28, quoted in N. Mukherjee, *Op.cit* p. 91.

Large crowds of people thronged to the city of Madras in search of work and food. The government of Madras at first refused to interfere with private trade in food grains but later felt it was necessary to purchase from those who imported, for distribution among the famine victims.

In 1823, Punganur experienced such an acute famine that several ryots abandoned their lands without paying their rent as all their crops failed. The Zamindar was left with no other option than to borrow from the money lenders an amount of 700 pagodas (Rs. 24,500) at exorbitant rates of interest in order to pay the installments of his peishcush due to the government.[5] The period 1823-24 was a period of scarcity throughout the Presidency. The Commercial Resident at Masulipatam, on observing the rise of prices, has compelled certain local merchants to sell rice at fixed prices and also wrote to the Bengal government for an amount of rice to be sent to him on government account. When this was brought to the notice of the Government of Madras, it greatly censured the Commercial Resident, pointing that such proceedings were likely to create a famine rather than to relieve the existing distress. However, several deaths due to starvation took place, many children were abandoned by their parents and also there was a serious grain riot that took place in the town of Masulipatam. But the government could put down the riot by pressing the military.[6] A graphic description of the peoples' distress during this famine could be seen in the narrative of one Elijah Hoole, a Christian Missionary, who was on a visit to these areas:

> "Many of the houses of the natives were unroofed for the purpose of giving the old thatch as fodder to cattle in the hope of keeping them alive till the next rainy season. Men and cattle were to be seen lying dead everywhere."[7]

The human suffering in the southern parts of the Zamindari due to the famine in 1832 was such that the Zamindar, Pedda Chikka Royal decided to undertake the completion of the tank near Gundagal, started during the period of his father, Shankar Royal I. The Zamindar paid the laborers in grain stored in his personal granaries in his palace and elsewhere in the Zamindari.[8] The tank was subsequently named after the late Zamindar, Shankar Royal and even now is known as *Shankar Royal Cheruvu.* In 1833 the Government of Madras in consideration of the reduced 'circumstances' of the Punganur Zamindari, lowered the annual peishcush and fixed it at Rs. 51,000 to be increased on a progressive scale for twenty years when it finally reached the usual Rs. 63,000. This was in line with the concessions given to Guntur Zamindars during the same period due to severe famine there.

What is generally known as 'Guntur Famine' occurred during 1832-33. Though many parts of Madras Presidency were affected, the entire district of Guntur was worst hit, hence the name, "Guntur Famine". It was also euphemistically called as *"Doccala Karuvu*" (It is said that there were instances when people never hesitated to rip open the bosom of others to snatch the food they had consumed). Between 1832 and 1835, the population of the district decreased by nearly one half, and more than two thirds of the livestock was lost. An eye witness had recorded the severity of the famine thus:

> "Hundreds die daily, literally of starvation........and although a strong body of police is constantly employed in collecting the dead.... Number of bodies are left to be devoured by dogs and vultures. Scorching wind and burning heat accompanied this terrible drought; and it was followed by plague and cholera. A man in perfect health was hardly to be found anywhere."[9]

The government stepped up relief by granting remissions in the payment of taxes. Efforts were made to contain the exodus of the people from the district as the government felt without people, land could not recover. Work on irrigation canals, tanks, roads and other public works was provided. The Zamindari of Guntur - Repalle, Sattenapalle, Chilakaluripet, Vasireddy and Malraju were not able to pay the stipulated peishcush as they could not collect any land revenue from the ryots. The Government of Madras therefore decided that the arrears of such peishcush should be lowered and after a considerable gap, a progressively increasing scale of peishcush was fixed until the Zamindari were restored to normalcy.[10]

It was the kind of concession given to the Guntur Zamindaries that was extended to Punganur Zamindari when the peishcush was lowered and a progressive payment was allowed for a period of twenty years. The 1832-33 famine also affected the southern Maratha area, Mysore, Hyderabad, Gujarat, Khandesh and also several parts in North India.

The next famine witnessed in Punganur was in 1854 when several parts of Madras Presidency were affected. Bellari District particularly was hard hit. Parts of Nizam dominions experienced severe famine conditions. An area of 30,000 square miles comprising a population of three million was affected during this famine. Wages for the labour were lowered so as to provide employment for larger population. It was reported that a great number of cattle also perished during this famine. Incidentally this was the last of the famines which occurred under the Company administration.[11]

The famines during 1800-60 phase interestingly did not evoke great concern for the government as there was not any specific policy for providing relief except for the District Collector giving occasional remissions in the payment of land taxes. The concessions given to the Zamindar in the payment of peishcush was not directly related to the relief for the peasants. The fixing of the progressive scale of peishcush is indicative of the rigidity in the system of Permanent Settlement which at that time was preferred by the government as against the Ryotwari, mooted by Thomas Munro.

Though the Zamindar was not granted a permanent Sanad and was kept on temporary leases, his administration has taken up works like digging of wells and tanks in the Zamindari. Government works in the initial stages were limited to providing earth digging work with a view to give purchasing capacity to the poor. As money was not to be doled out for nothing, the laborers were asked to dig the earth at one place and carry it to a distance and put it as a heap. Such steep mud heaps remained for several decades in the vicinity of Punganur and Madanapalle, as mute testimonies to the suffering of the people and as proof of the absence of any Famine Relief policies on the part of the government of the period. In a way, this was the phase when 'no policy' was the policy of the government.

Notes

1. N. Mukherjee, "The Ryotwari System and the Famine Problem in the Madras Presidency, 1792-1827" in V.K. Bawa (Ed.) *Aspects of Deccan History*, Hyderabad, 1975, p. 82.

2. *Ibid.*, p. 82.
3. Revenue Consultations, 16 July, 1804, Vol. 135, p. 1934.
4. Letter from Robert Ross, Principal Collector of Cuddapah to the BOR, 22 September, 1811, Cuddapah District Records, (C.D.R.) Vol. 653, A.P. State Archives.
5. Petition of Immadi Chikka Royal (Alias Nana Sahib), the Zamindar of Punganur to the Collector of Cuddapah, quoted in Letter from Dalzell, Acting Collector of Cuddapah to the BOR, 17 December, 1830, in C.D.R. Vol. 4579, p. 521. APSA.
6. Dalzell, *The Madras Famine of 1866,* quoted in N.Mukherjee, Op.Cit. p. 92.
7. Elijah Hoole, *Personal narrative of a Mission to the South of India, 1820-1828*, Part II, p. 219.
8. Petition of Pedda Chikka Royal to the collector of Cuddapah, 15 August, 1832, CDR, Vol. 4608, p. 381.
9. Col. Walton Campbell, *My Indian Journal*, quoted by Robert Eric Frykenberg, *Guntur District, 1788-1848*, Oxford, 1965, p. 2.
10. Robert Eric Frykenberg, *Op.Cit.* p. 140.
11. H.S. Srivastava, *The History of Indian Famines, 1858-1918*, Agra, p. 27.

VI

Famines During 1860-1870

By 1860 there were changes in the government policy in providing relief to the victims of famines in the Presidency. However, the wages varied from one district to the other. For example, wages in the entire North Arcot District were paid in cash though the amounts did not increase in commensurate with the increase in prices of essential commodities. The male coolie was paid 2 annas (16 annas made one rupee) and a female coolie was given 1 anna per day during the cultivation season. But the laborers in Kurnool and Cuddapah were slightly better off as they could find work on K.C. canal project where ordinary laborer working with his wife and children was paid between 12 annas and 1 Rupee per day.[1]

On 4 December 1865 there was a powerful hurricane for about 6 hours from midnight when there was great damage caused in the entire district of North Arcot. (Punganur was by then transferred from Cuddapah to North Arcot District). There were breaches to several channels. Railway properties at Nellore and Arcot were damaged. The damage to gardens, orchards and Areca nut trees as well as to house property was great.[2]

The famine familiarly known as *Ganjam Famine* of 1866 during which northern most parts of the Presidency like Ganjam

District, had its impact on the Punganur Zamindari.[3] Due to the failure of rains, the standing crops began to wither. J.D. Robinson, the Collector of North Arcot, wrote to the Board that the people in the western part of the district were facing acute food shortage. He further wrote on the condition of the famine stricken people thus:

> The needier classes are subsisting for several days in a week on roots, prickly pear and such like substitutes.[4]

The failure of rains also resulted in the scarcity of pasture and water for cattle. In Palamaner taluk, to the east of Punganur, the poor ryots drove their cattle to the neighboring Mysore jungles for pasturage.[5] Cattle diseases like Vakkai and Murrai broke out, and cholera was also reported as prevalent in several parts of the North Arcot district.[6]

Conditions improved by September with 'light and partial rains,' and by October there were 'steady rains' throughout the hill ranges on the western frontier. Cholera and the cattle diseases abated and the condition of crops was reported as 'improved and generally well' by November 1866.[7]

The period was very hard for the people of the Zamindari. By June there was a steep rise in prices of grain. The drought was severe and the standing crops started to dry up. Few crops like *Arikalu, Samalu, Cambu, Ragi* and *Cholam* under wells alone were active.

The 1866 Ganjam famine severely affected the Punganur Zamindari. In reality, it impacted the whole of Deccan involving a large portion of the eastern coast of India from Madras upwards, the entire Telugu speaking Districts, several parts of Mysore, Hyderabad dominions and Bombay were also affected during this famine. It is said this was the severest famine after John Lawrence (1864-69) became the Viceroy. In fact, the Ganjam Famine passed through two stages. The drought of 1865 caused a loss of nearly 70 percent of the rice crops. Local warnings like the price rise were ignored and no precautions were taken. For example, G.N. Barlow, the District Magistrate of Puri wrote to Revenshaw, the Commissioner of Orissa of the rise in prices and even suggested the need of checking it. But when the famine occurred, the authorities were thoroughly unprepared for the situation. Ganjam district in Madras Presidency recorded the maximum number of deaths during this famine.

The second stage in the Ganjam Famine was due to the unprecedented rains in the same year. This made the transport of food grains impossible both on land and by sea. Though some relief was organized, only a half of the stocks could reach the needy. Even in Madras, the prices of grain rose considerably. It was considered as the least efficiently and most extravagantly managed famine in the Presidency.

Even in Madras, the prices of grain rose considerably during the Ganjam Famine. Forbes, the District Magistrate reported that the people were forced to eat wild roots and plants and that migrations were rampant. It was suggested as early as February, 1866, that rice should be imported into Madras to meet the scarcity, but the proposal was rejected by the Government of Madras. However, the Government of India instructed the Provincial government to spend whatever sums were necessary for the relief of the people.

A Commission to examine the whole question of Ganjam Famine under the chairmanship of George Campbell was appointed by the Government of India. The Commission after visiting various affected places in the Presidency and after examining the witnesses, submitted its report in three parts. The first part dealt with the progress of the Ganjam Famine and the last two parts dealt with the recommended remedial measures. It is interesting to note that the Commission felt that the intensity of the famine was due to the failure to forecast developments, bad communication facilities, lack of irrigation and similar other reasons.[8]

In the Punganur Zamindari, by the early August 1866 though there was no indication of any onset of rains and the condition of the cattle also remained without any improvement, by the end of the month there was marked improvement in the general conditions as there was heavy rain on the night of 21 August 1866. It brought a great respite and the prospects of the season improved. Yet as the Collector reported that Cholera and cattle diseases still continued.[9] But in the next two months conditions further improved due to light and partial rains. Kangundi, Palamaner and Punganur received heavy downpour of rain and there was steady monsoon by October end. In few places due to heavy rains, some tanks also breached. Cholera and the cattle diseases also abated. On 15 November the Collector in his fortnightly report indicated that the cattle diseases disappeared and the condition of crops was generally well.[10]

Though 1867 appeared to be better, the next year again witnessed scarcity and near famine conditions. In his fortnightly report the Collector wrote to the Board about the failure of rain and added:

> The standing crops at all stages of maturity look stunted and sickly. Springs in wells are lower than they have been for very many years. Pasture may be said to have totally disappeared in the more open parts of the District.[11]

The conditions did not improve even by May that year. But in June as the Acting Collector Vans Agnew reported, there was steady improvement due to good rains and most tanks received supply varying from 1 to 3 months. The markets were well supplied, the prices were steady and the public health was "generally good". Though the cattle diseases like Murrain were not completely gone, there was improvement in pastures for cattle. The Collector also asked for discontinuing the fortnightly reports. But the Board of Revenue felt that such reports were to be sent once in month instead of fortnightly.[12]

However by November the situation became worse and the Collector wrote that due to failure of the monsoon the stocks of grain were lower and the resources of the people were less. Yet the Collector hoped that the situation may not deteriorate due to good communications. He wrote further:

> But I am satisfied that from series of bad seasons and consequent short productions, the resources of the bulk of the people are at so low an ebb that, without largely increased production, very considerable state aid would be necessary to enable the poorer classes to supply themselves with a sufficiency of imported food.[13]

As the Collector remarked in his report that the entire area "was now in a worse state than at the same period last year". The Board called for explanation of the meaning of the expression. Agnew had to further explain that he only meant that the situation was worse than it was before.[14]

This period also has seen severe famine that affected Central India as far as Jhansi and the Hissar division of Punjab besides Rajaputana. In the Bombay Presidency, the Districts like Poona, Ahmadnagar, Khandesh and Kaira were worst affected. In Madras Presidency, Cuddapah and North Arcot district in which Punganur was a part, were affected as stated .[15]

Two years later, in 1868 there occurred another famine throughout the North Arcot district that affected the people and the cattle. By February, the prices of food grains started to rise. Pasture and water failed particularly in all the highland taluks of Palamaner, Punganur and Kangundi.[16] About the condition of the crops and irrigational sources in the entire

Zamindari, the Collector wrote to the Board and the wording of the report is on the same lines of the earlier reports on the prevailing situation.

> The standing crops at all stages of maturity look stunted and sickly. Springs in wells lower than they have been for very many years. Many wells in all parts of district quite dry. Crops under wells dropping owing to insufficient irrigation. Pastures may be said to have totally disappeared.[17]

Acute scarcity continued up to June when there were some rains and most of the tanks received fairly good supply. The grain was available in the markets and consequently, the Collector also was asked to discontinue the sending of the Fortnightly reports.[18] The conditions considerably improved within 4 or 5 months and the Collector in early April 1869 reported that *Ragi* and *Cholam* (Jonna) were harvested in abundance in Palamaner and all along the western highlands of the district and as "these grains form the great staple food in those parts, the condition of the laboring classes there, is better than it has been for years".[19]

The Board of Revenue recommended for the postponement of the payment of peishcush due by the Zamindar on account of the famine conditions in the Zamindari. Orders were also passed by the Government on a letter from the Collector who on the recommendation of the Famine Officer-in-Charge of the Zamindari permitting the postponement of the repayment of the loan of Rs. 20,000 granted to the Zamindar of Punganur until after he has paid arrears of his pieshcush.[20] This loan was granted to him for the purpose of carrying out relief works in his estate during the years 1877-78.[21] However in 1881 the Government of Madras considering that Punganur Zamindari had suffered extremely during the famine, waived its claim for the repayment of the loan.[22]

With regards to the arrears of peishcush, a sum of Rs. 46,564 including interest that was due to the Government, the Zamindar wanted a year's time to be repaid. The Zamindar wrote to the Collector that due to unfavorable conditions of the season, and the consequent impoverished condition of his tenants he was not able to recover arrears of rent from them. The Collector W.S. Whiteside then wrote favorably that in Punganur Zamindari the earlier north-east monsoon was a poor one and the subsequent south-west monsoon was a complete failure; and that the Zamindari was not fully recovered from the previous famine. The Collector after personally visiting the Zamindari found that the condition of the ryots was anything but encouraging and reported that the water in the wells has greatly gone down. The Collector also testified that the Zamindar was known to be "very respectable, generous native chief, loyal to the British Government and always anxious to pay the Government its dues with punctuality" recommended that the payment of arrears be postponed by about six months.[23]

It was around this time that the Zamindar of Punganur opened negotiations with one J.H. Morison of a well established British firm, *Masri Corbettt and Morison* on the question of leasing out gold mining rights of the Zamindari to a company in England.[24] The Zamindar felt that this would improve the financial position of his Zamindari. But this proposal was left out as there were none to take it forward with Morison in England. Had it been pursued, and if the proposal of the Zamindar was only successful, Punganur like Kolar Gold Fields (KGF) must have been metamorphosed into a viable economic zone and famines must have become things of the past.

Notes

1. J.D. Robinson to the Board of Revenue (hereafter BOR) 17 August 1865, Proceedings of Board of Revenue (hereafter PBOR) 20 November, 1865.

2. BOR proceedings No. 7870, dt. 8 December 1865, p. 7041.
3. Ganjam (now in Orissa State), Bellary (in Karnataka), North Arcot (in Tamil Nadu), Kurnool, Cuddapah and Nellore (all in Andhra Pradesh) with a population of 6 million were affected during the famine in1866. As Ganjam was the worst hit, this famine came to be called as 'Ganjam Famine.' See B.M. Bhatia, *Famines in India*, Bombay, 1963, pp. 73-74.
4. Season Report of J.D.Robinson, Collector of North Arcot district, for 1 to 15 July, 1866 in BORP, 23 July 1866, No. 5068.
5. *Ibid.*
6. For details of the State of the season, see the Collector's Reports in BORP, 15 June, 1866, No. 4132, p. 4032. BORP, 21 August, 1866, No.5955, p. 5419 and BORP, 10 September, 1866, No. 6469, p. 5828.
7. J.D. Robinson's Fortnightly Reports to the Board of Revenue, in BORP, 5 October, 1866, No. 7152, p. 6349, BORP, 22 October, 1866 No. 7616, p. 6659 and BORP, 26 November, 1866, No. 8514, p. 7294.
8. H.S. Srivastava, The History of Indian Famines, 1858-1918, Agra, 1968, Pp. 87, 88. It may be noted that Sir George Campbell, later was appointed as Governor of Bengal.
9. BOR proceedings 10 September, 1866, No. 6469, p. 5828.
10. BOR proceedings 5 October, 1866, No. 7151, 22 October, 1866, No. 7616 & 26 November, 1866, No. 8514.
11. Robinson's letter, BOR proceedings 28 March, 1868, No. 2303, p. 2229.
12. G. Vans Agnew Acting Collector to Board, 9 June, 1868, No. 4374, p. 4067.
13. BOR proceedings 3 November, 1868 No. 7830.
14. *Ibid.*
15. N.T. Abraham, et.al, Economic History, Bombay, 1972, p. 88.
16. J.D. Robinson, Fortnightly Report, up to the end of February, 1868 in BORP, 10 March, 1868, No. 1779, p. 1642.
17. Vans Agnew, Acting Collector of North Arcot district to the BOR, 31 March, 1868. See BORP, 8 April, 1868, No. 2697, p. 2713.

18. Season Report for the week ending 8 June, 1868 from Vans Agnew to BOR. See BORP, 9 June 1868, No. 4374, p. 4067.
19. Letter from Vans Agnew to the Secretary, BOR, 23 October, 1868, in BORP, 3 November, 1868, No. 7816, p. 7830.
20. Retain Disposals (hereafter RD) (Revenue) 15 January, 1877, No. 133, RD 29 January, 1878 F.R. No. 231 & BOR Mis., 23 September, 1879 No. 8880, p. 9008.
21. BOR 26 June, 1878, No. 5917, p. 6436.
22. BOR 23 February, 1881, No. 357.
23. BOR proceedings 4 October, 1881, No. 2115.
24. *Ibid.*

VII

The Great Famine: 1876-78

Whenever there was a famine in any part of the Rayalaseema area, it had its echo in the Punganur Zamindari without exception. But all these cannot be compared in their intensity to the Great Famine of 1876-78 which had devastating effects on the people of the Zamindari. The Great Famine, *Pedda Karuvu* of 1876-78 also known locally as *Dhatu Karuvu* for, it started in the Hindu year *Dhatu*, affected a large part of British India, south of the Vindhyas. It was also known as Madras Famine as most parts of the Madras Presidency was severely affected by it. Besides Madras, the areas affected by this famine were Mysore, Hyderabad, Bombay and even North-West Provinces. The areas and the population affected most during this famine were as follows:

Table 7-1

Province	*Area in sq. miles*	*Population*
Madras	83,800	1,94,,00,000
Mysore	27,000	51,00,000
Hyderabad	30,000	19,00,000
Bombay	64,000	1,00,00,000

Source: Report on History of Famines in H.H. Nizam's Dominions in 1876-77, by Maulvi S.M. Ali, Para 26.

Of the 21 districts in Madras Presidency, as many as 14 including North Arcot, to which Punganur then belonged, were affected.[1] According to R.W. Fraser, an ICS officer, who worked as a lecturer in Telugu and Tamil for some time at London University: " To those who lived in South of India during 1876 and 1877 the memory of those years will ever be associated with the wave of desolation of famine which swept away 5 and a half million population who died in silent suffering notwithstanding all efforts made to save them."[2] The famine lasted for two years "during which not a single drop of rain fell and the total death rate for British India was estimated as far the largest number of people.[3] The Punganur Zamindari sustained a loss of nearly 1/5 of its population.

The failure of three successive monsoons, drying up of crops, high prices of agricultural produce, meager wages for laborers, scarcity of food grains etc., aggravated the sufferings of the people during the two dreadful years of famine. Adding to these general causative factors, the peculiarly unfavorable position of Punganur for free and quick transport as it stood isolated above the ghats, poor soil, precarious sources of irrigation-all considerably added to the existing agony.

About a year before the outbreak of the famine in 1876, Punganur, as in the other parts of Ceded Districts, experienced excessive rains. In three days ending with 21 October, 1874, as much as 20 inches of rain was recorded in so near a place like Madanapalle. All the tanks near the river channels breached and the crops failed. From the early 1876, those tanks which did not breach previously started drying up for lack of rains. Cultivation suffered the food grains became scarce and the prices began to soar. As the famine increased in intensity and before any relief could be given by the Zamindar or by the Government in the form of relief-works etc., "the starving people devoured the leaves of the *devadaru* and the pith of the aloe- both of which they cooked into a kind of broth," These brought on a virulent kind of diarrhea which in turn caused enormous deaths. Starvation deaths became common. About such deaths, F.A. Coleridge who as the Sub-Collector of Madanapalle had heard the eye witness accounts from one of his predecessors, J.D.B. Gribble, described thus:

> Corpses were to be found on every furlong of road – men, women and children in a perfect state of nudity being devoured in broad daylight by packs of jackals.[4]

Such deaths, Coleridge wrote, were very extensive along the roads to Gurrumkonda in Madanapalle taluk and Sadum in Punganur Zamindari. With the soil baked hard as a rock and the coolies unfit for protracted work for digging pits, it was not possible even to give a proper burial to the corpses of the famine victims.

It was during this period that there were reports of the peasants' riots due to non availability of food grains in some parts of south India. The deterioration of general economic conditions, over assessment of revenue, and the extortions of money lenders have caused riots of peasants in Supa, a village in Bhimitari taluk in Poona District early 1876. These riots soon spread to Ahmadnagar and other places and are well known as *Deccan Riots*. These riots though suppressed by the government, gave a warning of the serious decline of the economic conditions of the people. The passing of the Deccan Agriculturists Relief Act of 1879 by the government was the result of those riots.

Relief Measures by the Zamindar

The people residing in the Government Taluks of the North Arcot District had the benefit of the relief works started by the Government earlier than in the Punganur Zamindari. Consequent on the report of the Collector, W.S. Whiteside, about the disastrous state of the season as a result of the failure of the North-east and South-west monsoons and the imminent water famine throughout the district, the Board directed the Collector to prepare at once a scheme of works in consultation with the District Engineer to be undertaken to provide employment for the poorer classes.[5] Relief works by the Government were started throughout the District with a view to prevent crime which was common during times of scarcity. Though 2/3 of the total land revenue from Punganur went to the Government's treasury every year in the form of peishcush paid by the Zamindar, the Government took one full year to start any relief work in Zamindari.[6]

The Zamindar, Sankar Royal II in the meantime took whatever was possible within the reach of his ability and finances to alleviate the sufferings of the people in his Zamindari. On the outbreak of the famine, the Zamindar instructed his revenue staff to stop collection of land revenue from the peasants, opened a *langarkhana* (Poor Home) at which he daily fed 150 persons and on Monday which was the Shandy day as many as 400. This was incompatible to the enormous suffering experienced by the people. The Collector who had traveled throughout the Zamindari after the onset of the famine, wrote to the Board in November, 1876 that the crops have completely perished and the "deepest distress is now experienced by a large portion of the people."[7]

The Zamindar whose treasury became empty on the suspension of revenue collections on one side and on the expenditure of the poor home, had no recourse than to apply to the Government for a loan. The Article 4 of the *Sanad* issued on 1 Feb. 1861 to the Zamindar specifically points out that it was the duty of the Zamindar to provide relief to the people under his jurisdiction.[8] But the magnitude of the Great Famine was too heavy for the Zamindar to combat it all by himself with his limited resources. The Zamindar in his application to the Board of Revenue for a loan of Rs. 50,000, explained how he endeavored to give assistance as far as his resources permitted. He said that he not only owed over Rs. 5000, on account of the previous year's peishcush but expected that the current year's peishcush would be in excess of what he was expecting from his ryots. He expressed his desire to start relief works at once only if he had money. He wrote that "it grieves me to see them (poor ryots) starving" and pointed out the relief works carried on in the neighboring Government taluks. He further wrote:

> You (the Collector) will also be aware of the great distress that the inhabitants of my Zamindari are suffering; but along in the neighboring Government district (Cuddapah) relief works are now being carried on all sides, I to my great regret find myself utterly unable from want of funds to give my ryots any assistance whatever and I greatly fear that their distress will therefore continue to increase, and that possibly before the next cultivation season a number may die.[9]

The Collector while endorsing the Zamindar's letter recommending to the consideration of the Board pointed out the "bonafide manifestation of the Zamindar's anxious desire" to provide relief to the poor. He also pointed out that the same anxiety was not shown by the other great Zamindars of the district in spite of his efforts to 'stimulate them by letters urging them to evince some sense of their obligations in this respect.' The Collector contented that he was aware of the Government order prohibiting loans to private individuals or Municipalities under the provisions of Act XXVI of 1871. But, he said this has to be reviewed in the case of the Zamindar of Punganur, of whom he said:

> We have the case of a liberal-minded and very charitable landed proprietor, whose estate is suffering from famine as grievously as any of the adjacent districts; and who is

absolutely debarred by pecuniary difficulties from providing his starving tenantry with food, as is now being done by Government in so many places around him.[10]

Though the Collector felt that the amount Rs. 50,000 asked by the Zamindar as loan was necessary, he recommended that at least Rs. 30,000 be granted to him for relief works. He assured that the money would be spent under his supervision and the amount would be repaid in installments as soon as the conditions improved.

Even before the loan was granted, the Zamindar prepared a list of relief works mostly irrigation works to the tune of Rs. 20,000 that he wanted to undertake and submitted to the collector along with their estimates. The list contained 30 items of relief works. In that, 23 items were related to the earth work of various tanks all over the Zamindari. Among them the repairs on Ramasamudram and Pungamma tanks were shown to be Rs. 3,000 each. All other works on tanks and wells ranged from Rs. 100 to Rs. 1,500. The Zamindar wanted to sell grain at subsidized rates and the loss expected from such a sale was put at Rs. 1,500. The poor feeding at the *Langarkhana* was also estimated at an equal amount. The list submitted by the Collector was related to the road works all over the Zamindari. The Board submitted both the lists to the Government and they were duly approved in January 1877. The grant of loan to the Zamindar of Punganur served as a precedence to two other Zamindars in the North Arcot District, Karvetinagar and Kalahasti who also applied for loans for famine relief works. However, the Government refused to advance loans to them. But the Collector was asked to send proposals for granting them advances under the Land Improvement Act, that too if the Collector 'thought it desirable.'

The loan granted to the Zamindar was utilized as per the proposals sent earlier on the irrigation sources like cleansing of the tanks and digging of wells. The repairing of the bund of the Sankar Royalpet tank which originally was not included in the list was later added in a supplemental list. The Government sanctioned the estimated Rs. 500 and directed that the amount spent on the repairs be added to the loan already given to the Zamindar. Of the great concern shown by the Zamindar to provide relief to the people in his Zamindari, Benjamin Hitken, Special Correspondent of the *Statesman*, Calcutta, wrote when he visited Punganur in 1877 to see the extent to which the famine was affecting the people. He wrote:

> The Rajah (Sankar Royal II) himself has taken me over the town and to the principal relief works. He is struggling nobly to mitigate the distress of his people and I confidently hope that God will reward his habitual hospitality and large hearted sympathy with a blessing.[11]

Government Relief Works

Though the Government stepped in late to mitigate the sufferings of the famine stricken poor in the Zamindari, it did provide relief in more than one way. Immediately on the failure of rains and the drying up of tanks throughout the North Arcot District, the Collector W.S. Whiteside permitted the ryots to raise cucumbers, melons and pumpkins in the tank-beds without rents. He wrote to the Board that 'these crops does not involve in any great disturbance of the surface of the tank-beds and therefore were not injurious to the tanks.' As there was always a great demand for those vegetables and fruits from all classes of people during the hot season and as they grow quickly and luxuriously in the tank-beds, the Collector felt that such a cultivation would be a boon and great assistance to the ryots.[12] The Board immediatcly accepted the Collector's proposal and observed in their proceedings that the grant of special concession to grow vegetables in tank-beds was approved.

The Government of Madras towards the close of 1876 asked all the Collectors to direct the District Engineers to discontinue building operations and to give more importance for 'general employment on famine relief works.'[13] The Collector W.S. Whiteside pointed out to the Board how the ryots throughout the district were 'at their wits end to provide water for their own use or to keep their cattle alive,' and requested to authorize all the Tahsildars in his district to grant small advances to ryots under the Land Improvement Act.[14] The Collector also got approved of his proposal to suspend the collection of arrears of toddy rents in the entire district in view of the disastrous nature of the famine.[15] The Government in early 1878 directed the Collector to see that due attention was given in the distribution of clothes to the poor in relief camps in the Punganur Zamindari.[16] The Board also frequently made enquiries about the measures the President of the local Board of North Arcot District proposed to take in order to improve the famine conditions in Punganur.[17]

But the greatest relief came from the numerous road works which the Government undertook throughout the Zamindari as a part of their relief measures. Whiteside, the Collector, while submitting the list of relief works proposed by the Zamindar to the Board, also sent in a separate list, prepared in consultation with the District Engineer to undertake relief works, the expenses of which were to be met by the Government. The list contained 11 items of which 10 related to road works and one was about digging of a well in the *Pungamma Tank*. The new roads taken up were to a total extent of 64 miles, and this was apart from the road works in the Punganur town. The total estimated cost for the above roads was Rs. 37,000.[18]

The importance of undertaking road works in the Punganur Zamindari as a part of relief strategy by the Government was commensurate with the desired policy of the Government of

Madras in this regard. The Board in October, 1878 reflecting the Government views had observed:

> Considering the extent to which roads deteriorate when not properly attended to and the heavy outlay which will eventually be required to restore neglected roads to a state of thorough repair, the Board would further recommend that in the case of roads which it is not expedient to regard as famine works, District Engineers may be authorized to proceed with repairs under the ordinary grant when they are satisfied that such a course is necessary to prevent deterioration.[19]

When the relief works were newly opened, the people in distress, flocked to them. People came in such large numbers that the roads had to be divided into sections with regular camps, supplied with sanitary establishments and water arrangements.[20] Within a week after the Government sanctioned the amount of Rs. 37,000 towards the roads in Punganur Zamindari as a part of the relief works, the number of coolies employed in such works was as follows:

Table: 7-2

Men	1648
Women	750
Children	748
Total	3146 [21]

Mr. Engledow who distinguished himself as a Famine Relief Officer in Madanapalle was sanctioned Rs. 60 per month to supervise the relief camp at Ramasamudram in Punganur Zamindari.[22] Later on as the famine conditions became acute and the Government's efforts to provide relief were intensified, many officers from Bengal were deputed for relief works in the entire Presidency. A special Famine Relief Officer, Major

E.W. Shaw was then exclusively appointed in the Ramasamudram range in the Zamindari to supervise relief camps. He submitted regular weekly reports to the Collector, who duly endorsed and sent them to the Government. These reports are replete with the unprecedented human suffering due to the distress conditions. Major Shaw's place was taken up towards the close of 1878 by C.G.E. Bandray and he remained in the Punganur Division for about ten weeks till 3 January, 1879.[23]

Sir Richard Temple's Visit

It was during the height of this famine that Sir Richard Temple, the Lt. Governor of Bengal visited Punganur as part of his tour of the Madras Presidency. Richard Temple, whose organization of relief measures during the Bengal Famine in 1873 had won universal approbation, was asked by the Government of India to tour the Madras Presidency and advise the authorities. He arrived at Kurnool on 14 January, 1877.[24] After visiting various places all over Rayalaseema he arrived at Punganur on 2 February, 1877 from Madanapalle, accompanied by the Collector, Whiteside. Sir Richard Temple was much impressed "to hear the expressions of high personal esteem which the Collector invariably uses in respect" to the Zamindar. About the devastating famine that he witnessed in Punganur, Sir Richard Temple had written thus:

> But while we enjoy the social pleasure of meeting in his (Zamindar's) own house a native chief so distinguished, we cannot but remember the calamity from drought and scarcity which hangs over the Zamindary of Punganur, together with the adjoining British territories. I am sure that the Rajah will play his part worthily in aiding the efforts of the Government and its officers to mitigate or to avert from the

> people, the dangerous consequences of the extraordinary disaster which had befallen the harvest in his quarter.[25]

In November, 1878, Mr. Thornhill, the first member of the Board of Revenue while on a tour of the North Arcot District, "passed through the Zamindari from North to South and he has observed the state of the country on his way."[26] The visits of Sir Richard Temple and Thornhill had disastrous consequences as far as the payment of wages for coolies in the relief camps was concerned. While wages for men, women and children, throughout the North Arcot District were 2 Annas; 1 Anna and 3 paisa; and 1 Anna respectively, in the upland taluks of Palamaner the wages were slightly higher by few paise as these taluks happen to be nearer to the Kolar Gold Fields ((KGF) which always held greater attractions for employment. The Collector informed the Board that in Palamaner he "paid each male coolie 2 annas and 6 paise, and a good number of people came to work." But when Thornhill visited the district and wanted the Collector to reduce the rate to 2 annas, "a large number of coolies at once, went away."[27]

During the famine, at several relief camps the coolies were paid in grain also. But this system had several drawbacks. The disadvantages of this system is well narrated by R.K. Puckle the Director of Revenue Settlement when he wrote:

> Some bags (of grains) arrive 10 percent short in weight and the contents are sometimes musty. Much weighment, measuring, drying, storing and watching is needed and when the coolies get the grain they have to barter a portion with local bazaar men for salt and other condiments.[28]

Famine was widespread

The effects of the Great Famine were widely felt all over the Deccan. In Bombay for example, by the end of March, 1877, death of several hundreds of people on the road- side was reported. Their bodies were left to be eaten by dogs and jackals as there were none to give them a decent burial. The *Madras Mail* wrote on the state of famine thus: "If the *London Illustrated Graphic,* had an artist here for a week, we could create a sensation all over England that would surpass the stir that was made about the Bulgarian atrocities."[29]

Reduced wages as recommended by Sir Richard Temple were introduced even in the Bombay Presidency. The number of relief works came down drastically after the introduction of *Temple wages*. There were protests of the poor peasants in Sholapur and other places. Dr. Cornish, Sanitary Commissioner of Madras, having come to know of the disturbances at Sholapur, officially protested against such reduction in wages, as in his opinion, the new wage rate was insufficient to keep the people in good health.[30]

The picture in Mysore was no different. Richard Temple's policy of reduced wages had severely affected the relief camps. In Hyderabad dominions, acute famine conditions prevailed during 1877-78 due to failure of rains. The prices of food grains went up steeply. The famine was very severe particularly in the Districts of Lingasur, Raichur, Sholapur Gulbarga, Naldurg and Bidar.[31] As a result, there was great influx of people from Hyderabad State to the neighboring Madras Presidency. In order to check such migrations, the Government of Madras ordered not to open any relief works in the areas bordering Nizam's dominions. The Viceroy Lord Lytton visited Madras in August 1877 and was greatly disappointed at the local administration in providing relief. In the first week of September, he also visited Mysore where again he found insufficient relief works and overcrowded poor homes. The Viceroy created a new famine code, established relief kitchens and the relief works there, were reorganized.[32]

Conditions steadily improved in the Zamindari by February, 1878. The price of rice (second sort) which recorded 8.20 seers a rupee in the last week of January, 1878 improved to 8.60 seers by 2 February (it's price in 1876, before the famine, was 18.26 seers a rupee). There was also scanty rainfall (.01 inches) in January in the entire district.

The special Relief Officer G.P. Clerk suggested as early as May, 1878 to close down the relief works in the Zamindari and to retain only one camp at Punganur. But on the intervention of the Collector, they were continued for some more months. The relief camp at Royalpet was closed in June, and the Camp Superintendent at Punganur, Scoffeld was transferred to the relief camp at Trichanur near Tirupati.[33] The relief camp at Chowdepalli in the Zamindari was amalgamated with the one at Punganur and by December, 1878 Major E.W.Shaw, Famine Relief Officer in Punganur Zamindari was sent back to the Military Department to which he originally belonged.

Government's Relief to the Zamindar

The Zamindar of Punganur was shown every consideration by the Government during the famine. His request for the postponement of the payment of peihscush was favorably conceded. Besides, he was singularly exceptional in being exempted from the repayment of the annual peishcush that was given exemption earlier. There was also great sympathy towards the Zamindar by the Collector and other officials who assessed the intensity of the damage that was done by the famine in the Zamindari.

1. Postponement of Peishcush

As per the provisions of the Sanad,(1861) the Zamindar was to pay the stipulated peishcush and was not liable for any reduction of the amount due to any natural calamities. Yet, the impact of drought and famine in the Zamindari was such that, the Government was prevailed upon by the Collector to give relief in the matter of payment of peishcush. In October, 1874 when many tanks in the estate breached owing to heavy rains as noted earlier, the Government enabled the Zamindar to repair several of the breached tanks, by granting a reduction of Rs. 9,000 from the peishcush.[34] After the Great Famine broke out, the Zamindar wrote to the Collector in November 1876 for remission of the peishcush due for that year, because of the entire failure of North-East monsoon of 1876-77. He pointed out that none of the tanks in the entire Zamindari received any supply of water and even the few crops raised were also lost due to drought. The Collector who had just then traveled through the Zamindari from its 'extreme north to the southern boundary,' and thus having had personally seen the amount of devastation of crops due to drought, wrote to the Board that every tank in the Zamindari was dry, cultivation was at a standstill and prices were at famine-rates. He wrote that the Zamindar was always liked and respected by his people to whom he was "extremely charitable". The Collector further pointed out that the Zamindar was hitherto always punctual in paying his 'heavy peishcush,' and that it was impossible for him to make any payments to the Government "except by raising loans from *Sowcars* at ruinous interest." The Collector pleaded with the Board that out of Rs. 73, 683 that was due from the Zamindar on the peishcush as well as the quit rent, 50% of it i.e., Rs. 36,840 might be reduced. The Collector also informed the Board, the request made by the Zamindar for a permanent reduction of the peishcush.

The Board in their proceedings observed that the Zamindar fully deserved the testimony of the Collector but pointed out that giving remission was against the principles of Permanent Settlement. The Board further pointed out;

> The owners of large estates must be educated to keep a margin to meet the reverses of bad years and this salutary lesson will never be learnt by them (Zamindars) if the principle of permanent settlement be violated.[35]

The Board however, showed some concession in the payment of peishcush due for that year. The Zamindar was allowed to pay for that year's amount in half installments, and the remaining in about three years without interest. The Government sanctioned the above recommendation of the Board and it was duly communicated to the Zamindar through the Collector. The Collector met the Zamindar personally, and the Zamindar pleaded his utter inability to pay any portion of his Pieshcush with such a most disastrous season prevailing in his Zamindari.[36] Thereupon, the Collector addressed a letter to the Board in May, 1877 explaining the stand of the Zamindar and pointed out how severe the famine was in Punganur. He wrote:

> The long continued drought in his Zamindari has completely crippled its resources and it is difficult to convey an idea on paper of the present miserable condition of the Zamindari. I have just traveled through the various parts of the division. The tanks are all completely dry and there has been a total failure of crops of every description in addition to serious losses of farm stock owing to the scarcity of pasture.[37]

The Collector, in view of the pitiable circumstances that existed in Punganur, recommended to the Board that the collection of the entire peishcush for the year might be deferred until the season improved, and that the Zamindar was allowed to pay the arrears at the rate of one-fourth *kisth* every year. The Board accepted the recommendation of the Collector and observed that 'the demand for the whole of the Punganur Pieshcush for 1876-77 suspended.' The Board permitted the payment of arrears spread over four years beginning with 1877-78. This was approved by the Government of Madras in the same month.[38] But neither the Board nor the Government said whether the Zamindar was to pay any interest over the installments of *kisth*. The Collector therefore wrote pleading for the exemption of any interest on the payments of arrears of peishcush. He also cited the precedence of the Zamindar of Kalahasti who was exempted on an earlier occasion from the payment of interest over his arrears.[39] The Board instructed the Collector that "interest should not be charged on the Punganur Zamindar for the arrears." The Zamindar paid the arrears so promptly that the Collector Whiteside was moved to write to the Board in early July, 1878 that the arrears due by him was only Rs. 4778-9-3 for 1876-77 and Rs. 1698-3-2 for 1877-78. "All the rest he paid in spite of the unprecedented difficulties experienced." He said that the Zamindar was making very laudable effort to clear off the arrears of Pieshcush.[40] Having come to know that the Zamindar of Punganur was permitted by the Board of Revenue as well as by the Government to pay the Peishscush due for 1876 in four successive installments, the Zamindar of Kalahasti sent a petition to the Board in February 1876 requesting to allow him to pay his arrears of peishcush similarly in four installments without interest. But the Board refused to allow so long a period like four years. Yet the Board authorized the Collector to suspend the collection of Peishscush for 1876 and to recover it in two installments without interest during 1878 and 1879.[41] Thus Punganur was the only exception where so much liberality was shown in the payment of peishcush during the famine years.

2. *Exemption to repay the loan*

The Zamindar at the height of the famine had applied for a loan of Rs. 50,000 but the Collector recommended that at least Rs. 30,000 be given in view of the relief works that the Zamindar intended to take up. Accordingly the Government sanctioned Rs. 30,500 (an additional amount of Rs. 500 was given for the repair of the bund of the Sankar Royalpet tank). Out of it, the Zamindar was actually advanced during the sixteen months from March, 1877 to June, 1878 a total amount of Rs. 26,800-8-0. An amount of Rs. 500 was repaid by the Zamindar in August 1877. Thus the outstanding loan on the Zamindar stood at Rs. 26,300-8-0.

By March, 1879, the Government ordered for the recovery of the loan granted to the Zamindar for relief purposes during the famine. In the meantime, the Zamindar represented to the Government of Madras that he was still in arrears to pay his usual Pieshcush and that the repayment of loan might be postponed for three years. The Board of Revenue and the Government of Madras acceded to the request of the Zamindar, and the Government of India also confirmed the proceedings of the Government of Madras permitting the postponement of the repayment of the loan granted to the Zamindar. The formal acceptance orders of the Accountant-General were duly communicated about the Government orders. The acceptance of the Government of India for the postponement of the repayment of loan by the Zamindar induced the authorities at Madras to know of the actual financial position of the Punganur Zamindari. The Government of Madras directed the Board of Revenue to review the whole question of the financial position of the Zamindari and to report. The Board then directed the Collector of North Arcot to furnish the details of the revenue collected by the Zamindar during the ten years preceding the Great Famine, the extent of the waste lands available for cultivation and the probable time within which such lands were likely to be brought under the plough.

The Collector in his report sent after six months, gave the details of the collections during the ten years before the famine and went on to prove that the average income of the Zamindar did not exceed Rs. 7,795 and that he had sustained a loss of Rs. 26,075 during the famine year 1876. This, the Collector said, fell short of the usual one fifth of total revenue which alone came up to Rs.21,148. He pleaded for great consideration on the part of the Zamindar whose Peishscush he said was heavy, and whose estate was devoid of any possible extension of cultivation.[42]

In view of the financial strain on the part of the Zamindar and due to the devastating famine that razed his entire Zamindari, the Government of India favorably accepted the recommendation of the provincial Government and as an exceptional case passed orders in May, 1881 writing off the loan of 'Rs. 20,000' given during the famine.[43] At this stage, the Accountant General, Madras brought to the notice of the Government of Madras that the loan outstanding was Rs. 26,300-8-0 and inquired whether the remaining Rs.6,300-8-0 should be recovered from the Zamindar.[44] The Government of Madras, resolved to write off the remaining 6,300-8-0 also as this amount was not shown to the Government of India by oversight.[45] The Government also felt that if that additional amount had been brought to notice earlier, it would have been included in the recommendation. The Government of India for whom a copy of the above proceedings was sent, endorsed the order that the total amount of loan was exempted from repayment.[46] Thus the Zamindar of Punganur was given a considerable relief by the Government.

3. *Remission of Peishcush*

Another concession the Government gave to the Zamindar was the remission in peishcush. The Zamindar while requesting the Government for the postponement of the repayment of the loan, also had made a plea that the peishcush which according to him was rather heavy, might be reduced. The Government of Madras, asked the Board of Revenue to review the whole question of the financial position of the Zamindar with reference to the amount of Peishscush assessed and to report, "whether reduction is called for in accordance with the established principles of Permanent Settlement." The Board in their proceedings directed the Collector to furnish the details of the revenue realized by the Zamindar during ten years before the famine, and asked whether any relief to the Zamindar was necessary. The Collector W.S.Whiteside, in his letter to the Board discussed in detail the financial position of the Zamindari. He forwarded to the Board the statements giving all the statistics about the revenue, the waste lands in the Zamindari, the expenses of the Zamindar, etc. The average revenue realized by the Zamindar during 10 years prior to the famine was Rs. 1,05,740 as against the total assets of Rs. 1,47,135. When the payments made to the Government on account of peishcush, quit rent, land Cess, the expense on *Maramat* to tanks, and the establishment charges were taken into account, the average income during the ten year period was only Rs. 7,795. (In 1876, the Zamindar incurred even a loss of Rs. 26,075). The Collector pointed out that the private expenses of the Zamindar were about Rs. 32,000 per year which according to him was "by no means excessive considering his position and dignity." As the average income Rs. 1,05,740 was nearly Rs. 41,395 short of the total assets of Rs. 1,47,135, the Collector pleaded that the peishcush also be reduced by one-fourth in relation to the general fall of income. The Collector also compared the Peishscush of Punganur with other Zamindaries in the district like Kalahasti, Karvetinagar and Kangundi to show, how unfavorably the percentage of Punganur Peishscush on its assets was fixed. He spoke highly of the family of the Zamindar of Punganur which according to him "always been conspicuous for its faithful and loyal conduct towards the British Government from the earliest times." About the then Zamindar Shankar Royal II, the Collector said:

> He is the only landed proprietor in this (North Arcot) district which when the terrible pressure of the late famine began to be felt, evinced real anxiety for the condition of his ryots and volunteered to be responsible for the payment of the money that may be advanced by Government to save the lives of his starving people.[47]

The Collector therefore recommended that the future peishcush of the Zamindar to be fixed at Rs. 50,000 which was about 50 percent of the average annual revenue of Rs. 1,05,740.[48]

The Board in their proceedings contended that the peishcush on the average income was only 60 percent and that it was not higher than the proportion of the assets usually fixed as the revenue payable to the Government according to the established principles of the Permanent Settlement. The Board did not accept the views of the Collector in comparing the Punganur Peishcush with the Peishscush of the other Zamindaries in the district. It said that the peishcush for those Zamindaries was not fixed in relation to their assets but was 'on equivalent for the military service to which they were previously liable and thus not analogous to that of Punganur.' Yet the Board in view of the 'Zamindar's good conduct and public spirit as an act of grace' supported the recommendation of the Collector to reduce the peishcush to Rs. 50,000, and submitted the same to the Government.[49] But the Government of Madras in their order in February, 1881 refused to comply with the recommendations of the Board to reduce the peishcush amount as it amounted to violate the established principles of the Permanent Settlement.[50]

When the Government turned down the recommendation of the Board for a permanent reduction in the peishcush, the Zamindar tried to get at least postponement of the payments.

He wrote to the Collector in October 1881 requesting him to recommend to the Board as well as to the Government that he might be given a year's time to pay the arrears of peishcush without interest. The Zamindar stated that the unfavorable state of the season and the consequent impoverished condition of his tenants only made him impossible to collect the arrears of rent in his Zamindari.[51] The Collector W.S. Whiteside, writing from Palamaner to the Board within a week, pointed out that a sum of Rs. 46,564 was due up to the end of September, 1881 from the Zamindar. He said that the Zamindar was a "responsible, loyal and generous native chief, who was always anxious to pay the Government dues with punctuality." The Collector further stated that "the Zamindar was personally going about his Zamindari endeavoring to supervise collections of revenue but with very indifferent success." The Collector who had just then visited the Zamindari pointed out to the Board that how the conditions were far from satisfactory. He wrote:

> The Zamindari has not yet fully recovered from the effects of the late famine and there has been a succession of bad seasons. I have lately visited the estate and can from my own observation declare that the state of the country and the condition of ryots are anything but encouraging. There has been no rain whatever for dry cultivation and the water in the wells has greatly gone down.[52]

The Collector informed the Board that the Zamindar has opened negotiations with one J.H.Morison, of the firm Messrs. Corbett and Morison on the matter of leasing out the gold mining rights of the Zamindari to a Company in England. Morison who went to England was expected to make necessary arrangements in the matter. The Collector felt that if the scheme matured, the Zamindar of Punganur would have sufficient funds to pay up the arrears of peishcush. Therefore the Collector recommended that the Zamindar be granted six months time to pay the arrears with interest. The Board sanctioned the proposal of the Collector, and gave the Zamindar six months time to clear the arrears of peishcush with interest.

By the middle of 1882, the Zamindar again fell into arrears of payment to the tune of Rs. 53,245. The Collector A.J. Stuart who had succeeded Whiteside took very sympathetic view of the condition of Punganur and wrote to the Board in July, 1882 that the 'very high proportion of peishcush and the evil effects of the recent famine' (1876-78) have disabled the Zamindar to discharge his payments. He pleaded that some considerable remission or assistance was needed in his case. He further wrote:

> I think it highly desirable to abstain from adopting coercive measures against him (The Zamindar) until final orders are passed on my proposal as to press him now will be to throw him into the hands of the money-lenders and usurers, and by withdrawing all hope of extricating himself from his liabilities, lead to the ruin of a worthy and respectable gentleman.[53]

The Board then called for a detailed report on the Zamindari and the Collector submitted his report in September, 1882. The Collector discussed at length the great effects of the famine which ravaged the Zamindari in which about 20 percent of its population and a large number of cattle perished. This, the Collector said, had badly affected the financial position of the Zamindar as he could not collect the revenues from the ryots. About the position of the Zamindar, the Collector said:

> Though living in the most economical manner and paying all he can to the State, the Zamindar of Punganur has fallen into arrears to the extent of about half a lakh. He is unable to repair his palace, a portion of which is falling into ruins and has no money to keep up the numerous irrigation works in his Zamindari upon which his revenue largely depends.[54]

The Collector citing the details of the average collections in the Zamindari tried to prove how the peishcush was disproportionately higher to the income derived by the Zamindar. He earnestly wanted that as exceptional case, the Zamindar of Punganur should be given both remission of a portion of the demand which has fallen into arrears and also a reduction of the peishcush at least for a term of years extending to twenty or twenty five years, "until the Zamindar has time to recover from the effects of the famine." If such a concession was not given, the Collector pointed out that he will have no other option than to resort to coercive measures to recover the arrears. This, the Collector said will naturally result in the Zamindar borrowing money at exorbitant interest and this in turn, the Collector contented will ruin the estate.

The Board which was not convinced at the Collector's argument observed in their proceedings that there was no sufficient ground to believe that the peishcush was heavy and thus showed every aversion to reduce the peishcush. The Board also expressed the apprehension that such a reduction would give rise to similar claims from other Zamindars. But the Board took a considerate view of Punganur for having suffered from the famine and decided to write off the entire arrears due from the Zamindar. The Board observed:

> Considering however, that the present crippled condition of the Zamindari is entirely due to losses by famine and the expenses incurred by him in its relief, the Board recommended that the whole of the accumulated arrears, amounting, it is said, to about half a lakh of rupees should be written off. The Zamindar freed from the weight of debt will then be enabled to make a fresh start.[55]

The Government concurred with the Board and observed in their proceedings (22 January, 1883) that a permanent reduction of peishcush cannot be made. However, the

Government sanctioned the remission of arrears outstanding against the Zamindari.[56]

The Great Famine brought disastrous effects on Punganur Zamindari. Even today the entire region is replete with numerous folk songs that tell the ghastly ravages of the *Pedda Karuvu*. According to the Regulations of the Permanent Settlement, it was the duty of the Zamindar to provide relief to his people during times of famine. On his part, the Zamindar of Punganur undertook relief works like tank repair, poor feeding and grain distribution. But the magnitude of the Great Famine was such that the Zamindari finances alone could not mitigate the suffering of the people. The Government intervention became inevitable. Moreover, the Government received nearly 2/3 of the land revenue as peishcush from the Zamindar. Therefore, there was the ultimate moral responsibility on the part of the Government to come to the rescue of the Zamindar in his attempt to provide relief to the suffering.

Government took up mostly road laying works and establishment of *Langarkhana* or Poor Homes. Apart from providing relief to the poor, the Government also gave some concessions to the Zamindar. They included postponement of peishcush, writing off the loans and remission of arrears of Peishscush. These concessions shown to the Zamindar were aimed at bringing relief ultimately to the people of the Zamindari.

It is interesting to note that in the Hyderabad dominions, during the famine of 1876-78, as a part of the relief works, the Nizam's government appointed a committee with Maulvi Mehdi Ali to coordinate the relief measures. The Committee consisted of ten officials and seven non officials as members. This central committee was authorized to send special commissioners into the most affected districts in order to initiate measures of relief, subject to the sanction of the Maulvi Mehdi Ali Committee.[57]

The severity of the Great Famine all over the south was such that in May, 1878, the Government of India appointed the first ever Famine Commission with eight members under the chairmanship of Sir John Strachey, to go into the details of the unprecedented famine and to suggest ways and means to prevent such occurrences in future. The committee submitted its report in 1880 and this may be considered as a landmark in the history of Famine policies in India. The commission felt that the responsibility of the State was not to allow any one to die for want of food. Among other numerous suggestions the Commission made, village relief, remission of revenue, creation of Agricultural department, provision of irrigational facilities, extension of Railways, Forest conservancy, formulation of famine codes etc. were important. The famine policy adopted after this Report was either based on its recommendations or was influenced by it.[58] Thc good thing about the Famine Commission was that it was asked to look into the peculiarities of the individual provinces and assess the steps the provincial governments were initiating and gather statistics about the affected people, details of price rise of food grains; climate, rainfall patterns, soil, water, density of population, cultivation patterns and a host of such details. These details proved to be useful for the successive years for the government to take precautionary methods to address the scarcities without waiting for the famines to become severe.

Notes

1. C. D. Maclean, *Manual of the Administration of the Madras Presidency*, Vol.I, Madras, 1885, p. 300.
2. R.W. Frazer, *British India,* T. Fisher, Unwin, London, 1896, p. 333.
3. F.A. Coleridge, *A Brief History of Madanapalle*, Trichinopoly, 1911, p. 15.
4. *Ibid.*

5. W.S. Whiteside, Collector, N.A. District to the BOR, 10 January, 1876, See BORP, 18 January, 1876, No. 135, p. 249.
6. When the conditions deteriorated, the Government of Madras in their G.O. Retained Disposal (R.D.) No. 12189, 5 December, 1876 directed the Collector, North Arcot to take steps to "start relief works in Punganur Zamindari or its immediate neighborhood." See BOR Proceedings, 14 December, 1876, No. 11005, p. 127.
7. W.S. Whiteside to BOR, 7 November, 1876, See in BORP, 11 November 1876, No. 2810, p. 9069.
8. The Article 4 of the Sanad clearly pointed out that the remissions which were occasionally granted earlier as a custom "on account of drought, inundation or other calamity of the season, shall now cease and never be revived." The *Sanad-I-Mikeut Istimrar* or Deed of Permanent Property of Punganur Zamindari, 1861.
9. Letter from Sankar Royal, Zamindar of Punganur to the Collector of Chittoor to be endorsed to the BOR and the Government, 6 November, 1876, BORP, 11 November, 1876, No. 2810, p. 9071.
10. Whiteside to the BOR, 7 November, 1876, in BORP, 11 November, 1876, No. 2810, p. 9070.
11. Meer Mohammed Saheb, *Extracts of notes by European travellers in the books kept at the Palace of H.H. The Rajah Sahib*, C.I.E. of Punganur, Madras, 1884, p. 136.
12. Whiteside to the Secretary, BOR, See BORP, 10 March, 1876, No. 685, p. 2589. Under similar circumstances, the Collector of Cuddapah also permitted the cultivation of such vegetables and fruits. Their cultivation near Siddavatam was in so abundance that one type of water melon is mostly known as 'Siddavatam fruit.'
13. G.O., 2 December, 1876, (R.D.), No. 2876. See BORP, 9 December, 1876, No. 10837, p. 1006.
14. W.S. Whiteside, Collector of North Arcot to the BOR. See BORP, 12 January, 1877, No. 133.
15. BORP, 26 October, 1877, No. 4861.
16. BORP, 21 February, 1878, No. 1921, p. 1555.
17. BORP, 12 September, 1879, No. 8540, p. 8811.
18. Whiteside to H.E. Stokes, Acting Secretary, BOR, 23 December, 1876, No. 576. See BORP, 29 December, 1876, p. 10568.

19. BORP, 28 October, 1878, No. 2885, p. 9321. When the roads were in execution, the Government sanctioned the expenditure in excess of original grant incurred on earth-work of road from Sundupalle to Royalpeta. On the recommendation of the Collector, the Government also sanctioned additional expenditure on road from Punganur to Ramasamudram, but declined for the repair of road between Royalpet in Punganur division and Palamaner Trunk Road.
20. F.A. Coleridge, Op.Cit., p. 16.
21. Talukwar Abstract for the week ending Saturday, 6 January, 1877. See BORP, 12 January, 1877, No. 128.
22. Engledow also supervised a poor house *Langarkhana* at Madanapalle where relief to the poor and the abandoned children was provided. He was appointed after the famine to the Police Department. See BORP, 30 September, 1878, No.10017, p. 8744.
23. Meer Mohamed Saheb, *Extracts,* p. 104.
24. For details of the tour of Richard Temple in Rayalaseema and the instructions given to him by the Government see B.M. Bhatia, Op.Cit., p. 94.
25. Sir Richard Temple's note in the Visitor's Book at the Palace, Punganur. See Meer Mohammed Saheb, *Extracts*, p. 136.
26. W.S. Whiteside to the BOR, 18 November, 1876, in BORP, 29 November, 1876, No. 2997, p. 9542.
27. Whiteside to the Chief Secretary, 18 November, 1876. See BORP, 6 December, 1876, No.3092. The reduction of wages by Sir Richard Temple all over the Presidency also resulted in the fall of the number of coolies at the Relief camps. The reduced rates were familiarly known as the "Temple Rations." See B.M. Bhatia, Op.Cit., p. 95.
28. BORP, 26 December, 1876, No. 3287, p. 10465.
29. William Digby, *Famine Campaign in Southern India, 1876-78*, (Vol. I London) p. 95.
30. For a detailed discussion on the reactions to the Temple wages, see, H.S. Srivastava, op.cit, Pp. 133-34.
31. Zareena Praveen, Famine Relief Measures in Hyderabad State, A.R. Kulkarni et.al (Ed.), *History of Modern Deccan,* Vol. 2, Hyderabad, 2009, p. 120.

32. Lady Balfour, *Lord Lytton's Administration*, p. 210.
33. BORP, 22 October, 1878, No. 10794, p. 9294.
34. G.O., 12 June, 1875, No. 904, quoted in BORP, 29 November, 1876, No. 2997, p. 9542.
35. BORP, 29 November, 1876, No. 2997, p. 9543.
36. BORP, 4 June, 1877, No. 2575, p. 4607.
37. W.S. Whiteside to H.E. Strokes, Secretary, BOR, 25 May, 1877, quoted in BORP, 4 June, 1877, No. 2575, p. 6407.
38. G.O. (R.D.), 25 June, 1877, No. 2100.
39. W.S. Whiteside to the BOR, 31 January, 1878, No. 27 in BORP, 8 February, 1878, No. 338.
40. W.S. Whiteside to the BOR, 3 July, 1878, see BORP, 18 July, 1878, No. 1995, p. 6860.
41. BORP, 13 February, 1878, No. 384, p. 1274.
42. The total Revenue according to the Collector was Rs. 1,05,740 and 1/5 of it was 21,148 and thus the average income of the Zamindar fell short by Rs. 13,353. See letter from Whiteside to the Secretary, BOR, 21 May 1880, No. 210 in BORP, 12 August, 1880, No. 1148, p. 5108.
43. G.O. (R.D.), 9 June, 1881, No. 1560, quoted in BORP, 23 June, 1881, Mis. No. 6164, p. 3663.
44. Letter from the Accountant General to the Secretary, Revenue Department, Government of Madras, see BORP, 19 July, 1881, No. 1435, p. 4707.
45. Proceedings of Webster, Secretary to Government (Revenue), 2 July, 1881, No. 1010, in BORP, 19 July, 1881, No. 1435, p. 4707.
46. Letter from J.E.O.' Conor, Assistant Secretary, Government of India (Department of Finance and Commerce) to the Chief Secretary, Government of Madras, 10 August, 1881, No. 2267, See BORP, 13 October, 1881, No.2277.
47. Letter form Whiteside to the Secretary, BOR (Camp: Palamaner), 21 May, 1880, No. 210. See BORP, 12 August, 1880, pp. 5108-10.
48. *Ibid.*
49. BORP, 12 August, 1880, No. 1140, p. 5111.
50. G.O. 23 February, 1881, No. 357, quoted in the petition of Sankar Royal II, the Zamindar of Punganur to Frederick Temple, Viceroy

and Governor General of India, January 1885, See *A.S.R. Collections,* Vol. I, p. 2.

51. Letter from Sankar Royal, the Zamindar of Punganur to the Collector, North Arcot district, quoted in BORP, 4 October, 1881, No. 2115.
52. W.S. Whiteside to the Secretary, BOR, 19 August, 1881, (Camp: Palamaner). See BORP, Ibid.
53. A.J. Stuart, Collector of North Arcot, to the BOR, 21 July, 1882, No. 312. See BORP, 4 August, 1882, No. 1932.
54. A.J. Stuart, to the Secretary BOR, 24 September, 1882, No. 398. BORP, 16 November, 1882, No. 2808.
55. BORP, 4 August, 1882 No. 1933.
56. G.O. (R.D.), 22 January, 1883, No. 91. quoted in BORP, 6 February, 1883, Mis. No. 1050, R.O.S.A.T.
57. Zareena Parveen, "Famine Relief Measures in Hyderabad State", A.R. Kulkarni, et.al, (Ed), *History of Modern Deccan, op.cit,* p. 121.
58. K.S.S. Seshan, Famines and Relief Measures in the Deccan (1800-1947), A.R. Kulkarni et.al. (Ed), *History of Modern Deccan (1720-1948)* Vol. 2, 2009, Hyderabad, Abul Kalam Azad Oriental Research Institute, Hyderabad, p. 115.

VIII

The Famines During 1891- 1901

Punganur witnessed yet another bout of severe famine towards the end of the 19th century. Considered as the most severe of all the Famines in the Zamindari, this famine witnessed the untold suffering of both humans and cattle for want of food, water and fodder. During 1891-92, there arose a situation in Punganur when food scarcity became acute and famine returned to the entire Zamindari in full measure. Much of the information regarding this famine is available in the Fortnightly Reports of the Special Deputy Collector sent to the Board of Revenue.[1] While the famine was widespread even in the entire North Arcot District to which Punganur then belonged, it was very severe in Punganur due to utter deficient rainfall and the resultant crop failure.

As the season appeared to be quite unfavorable, the Zamindar of Punganur sent a petition on 4 April 1891 through the Collector to the Board of Revenue asking for remission of the amount of his Peishscush.[2] The Collector while submitting a report on the general prospect in the district in October 1891, pointed out that the rainfall in Punganur during that month was only 4.80 inches which was lowest in the district next only to Tirupati station where it was 4.75, while the district average stood at 8.07 inches. As for Punganur, the Collector said there was not a drop of rain in November as the big tank (Pungamma Cheruvu) near the town was absolutely dry. Ramasamudram division in the Zamindari extending over a tract of 300 square miles with a population of 58,793, was the worst affected.

The District Collector Le Fanu wrote on 19th November 1891 to the Board of Revenue stating that the western half of the Zamindari was in a bad condition and cautioned of the prospects of imminent famine in the Zamindari. To prove his point, the Collector furnished the rainfall statistics for the month of November and December from 1873 to 1890.[3]

Table - 8-1: Rainfall Statistics for Nov. & December

Year	*November*	*December*[4]
• 1873	.00	.00
• 1874	.40	.00
• 1875	.00	.55
• 1876	.35	.00
• 1877	3.20	.65
• 1878	4.90	.85
• 1879	9.15	.15
• 1881	4.14	.10
• 1882	10.84	.00
• 1883	13.28	3.55
• 1884	5.25	2.80
• 1885	3.50	3.70
• 1886	3.00	.30
• 1887	10.40	3.40
• 1888	8.50	.00
• 1889	.50	2.65
• 1890	3.00	.80

For the year 1891 up to the end of October it was 12.28 inches as against an average of 25.89 for final years during the

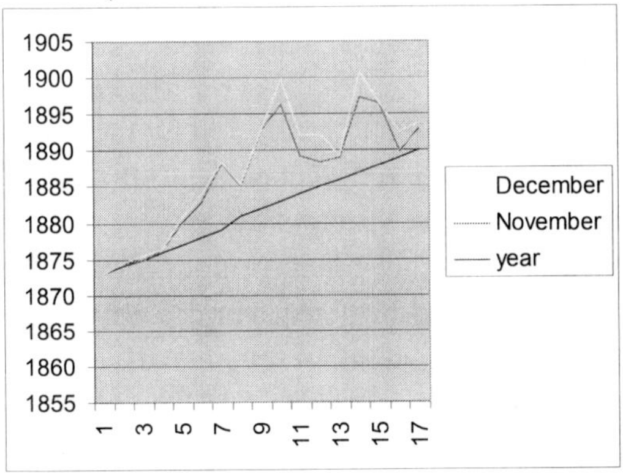

same period. Even this meager 12.28 inches occurred on 28 days over a period of 10 months. To further convince his line of arguments the Collector gave the rainfall statistics pertaining to the period April-November, 1891.[5]

Table 8-2

Months	*1891 (in inches)*	*Average of the previous five years*
April	0.50	0.91
May	0.55	4.50
June	1.78	1.59
July	1.40	3.10
August	1.90	3.53
September	1.35	4.96
October	4.80	6.28
November	0.60	5.15

The Board of Revenue however was not prepared to accept the alarmist view of the Collector which was based on the rainfall statistics. The Board stated that the North- East monsoon was not a phenomenon of frequent occurrence in Punganur. To stress its view point, the Board also furnished details of the rainfall during November and December of the previous 18 years, i.e. from 1873 to 1889. But the Collector Le Fanu stuck to his apprehensions that there was no way of escaping widespread distress.

The noticeable feature of the rainfall for the entire year, 1891 was capricious which even according to popular belief was characteristic of famine year. As there were no prospects for further rain, the long continued drought absolved what little supply of tanks received earlier. Several tanks became dry. Wet cultivation came to a standstill in several parts of the Zamindari. Pasture had become scarce. People started selling away their cattle in large numbers. It was said that about 1000 cattle died in a single village, Parvathinagar. It was estimated that more than 30,000 head of cattle must have died in the entire Zamindari. The Divisional Officer reported that collection of grass and fuel and few road works gave some work to laborers but that did not help a large number. The merchants started holding back their stocks in view of the threatening famine. The carts passing on the main roads were attacked and robbed by dacoits for grain. In Venkatagiri Kota, there was a torch light dacoity in which about twenty people took part. Another dacoity was reported near Somala. The dacoits have even attacked the party of a Deputy Collector when they were returning from Sodam. The dacoits were reported to have been mainly in search of grain and money. The Collector reported to the Board that the situation in Punganur was "critical."[6] The Collector also added:

> I fear that there is no hope of escaping widespread distress or rather that for the word "distress" which has hitherto been euphemistically used, the word "famine" must shortly be substituted.[7]

As to the provision of relief works, the Collector suggested that the PWD may draw plans for a Railway Branch line to join Kolar with Katpadi via Venkatagiri Kota, Punganur and Madanapalle. However, this scheme was not taken up.[8]

By January 1892, the condition in the Zamindari showed visible signs of scarcity due to monsoon failure. The Assistant Collector of North Arcot from his camp at Venkatagiri Kota reported to the Collector that the rains were scarce and that Punganur was passing through a tough time. There was no water in any of the tanks in the western part of the Zamindari and the cultivation has come to a standstill. Bengalgram and the water - melon were raised in the empty tank-beds. As there was no possibility of wet-cultivation, Cholam was sown on 'wet' lands. Ragi on dry lands yielded not more than ¼ of produce. Horse gram did not fare better. Though the markets were steady, the prices of grain were high. It was reported that rice was sold at 9 ½ local measures per rupee and Ragi at 16 measures (while the normal rate was 16.2 seer). The ryots had sufficient grains as stock, the poorer sections and coolies did complain of high prices. They felt the want of work and food. The Assistant Collector felt that they were not prepared to leave their houses in search of work. There were also crimes like grain looting, reported by then. It was proposed to start relief works in the western part of the Zamindari and the proposal was approved by the Board of Revenue.

By January 1892, there was no rainfall and so there was no supply of water in tanks. There was very little wet cultivation under tanks. As there was no water in the tanks, ryots started raising melons and Bengalgram on the tank-bed lands.[9] The situation grew worse as the area of wet land sown up to middle of December was 2,697 acres in the Zamindari, which was only 1/3 of the average of the previous 3 years. This amounted to 1/5 of the total wet holdings of 13,535 acres. Ninety percent of the Paddy crop has already or expected to fail entirely. The Collector reported that of the 12,000 acres of Ragi on dry lands, 10,000 acres was a total failure. The Commissioner of land Revenue visited Punganur on 15 January 1892 and held consultations with the Zamindar. He had observed how all the tanks were dry. The Collector also in his report to the Government marked out a rough sketch of the map of Punganur Zamindari, the portion which was hard hit. The marked portion was a tract with Punganur at its center covering an area of 300 square miles with a population of 58,793. The area and population of the entire Zamindari was 648 square miles and 91,852 souls.[10] In the above tract described as most affected, relief works pertaining to laying of the roads were taken up to provide work for at least 2,000 laborers. The Collector's proposal to the Board was favorably considered and the Accountant General was liberal to place Rs. 20,000 at the disposal of the Collector of North Arcot to start road works in the Punganur Zamindari.[11]

The Zamindar also applied to the Government for a loan of Rs. 10,000 without interest to enable him to restore irrigation works so as to provide relief to the distressed. The Collector having known the Zamindar's generous and charitable disposition towards the people, favorably recommended for the grant of the said loan. The Collector also pointed out that Punganur Zamindar was the only landed proprietor who volunteered to repay the money that was proposed to be advanced by the Government during the Great Famine of 1876-78. He also felt that the Peishscush on Punganur was such that it did not allow any accumulation to be made in ordinary years to meet reverses of bad years. The Collector added that Zamindar's "style of living is by no means extravagant". The Board accordingly recommended to the Government to sanction a loan of Rs. 10,000 to the Zamindar on a simple interest of 4 ½ percent, repayable in five equal installments.[12]

There were also several ryots in the Zamindari who wanted to obtain loans to dig wells. By February 1892, about 27 ryots have applied loans for about Rs. 5,000 in total. This was seen as a welcome sign by the district administration for, such works would provide relief nearer to the homes. Owing to the lack of rainfall in Punganur, the supply of drinking water in ponds and wells had run out as they became completely dry. There was need to deepen and repair them so that men and cattle will not have water-scarcity. The Collector was permitted by the Board to use the funds duly granted for relief.[13]

By March, the famine was so intense, that the Government was compelled to take up several works in the entire Zamindari to provide relief to the suffering poor. Six new roads of 15 miles length with an estimated cost of Rs. 20,720 and repairs for 13 old roads to a length of 19 miles at a cost of Rs. 1,25,396 were taken up. Apart from the road works, few other works for drinking water supply Rs. 8000 and for removal of prickly pear another amount of Rs. 17,000 was also taken up. The new works came to a total of Rs. 1,71,116.[14]

During the drought, the poorer sections were allowed to gather tamarind fruits freely in the forests. The eastern parts of the Zamindari viz., Sadum, Avulapalle, Nanjampet, Nayanapakala, Palamanda and parts of Kandur were slightly better when compared to the western parts. Of the 1212 tanks in the entire Zamindari 914 tanks became completely dry and in 272 tanks had supply ranging from 5 to 11 days. The grass cutting work at Ramasamudram was carried under the supervision of the Forest Department. A temporary forester was appointed to receive grass from coolies and pay at the rate of 2 annas for 50 lbs. This was carried on for 6 days a week; Sunday being a holiday.[15]

A poor house was opened at Ramasamudram on 12 March, 1892 with 2 men, 2 women and 28 children.[16] As the pasture became scarce, people resorted to digging pits in the tank-bunds and *vankas* A total of 153 tons of grass was collected up to

5 March and the amount spent was Rs. 2,190. In the month of February alone about 18 cattle deaths were reported in the Zamindari. The loss of cattle was heavy because the ryots look after the stall fed cattle alone and leave the emaciated to their fate. The Deputy Collector reported that "owing to want of fodder, cattle have gradually lost strength and in some places they do not rise again when once they lie down; but die a slow death."[17] The special Deputy Collector after a visit to Ramasamudram area described the plight of the cattle to the Board of Revenue as a first hand report. Based upon the reports of the Deputy Collector and then the Collector of the district, the Board of Revenue made the following resolution:

> The condition of the Zamindari remain unaltered. The scarcity of water is being met by deepening and clearing out the wells. Fodder is scarce and dear and what is available is reserved for the more valuable draught cattle, the rest being left to shift for themselves.[18]

Crops like Paddy, Sugar-cane, Jonna and Chillies under few wells and tanks where there was water, were in fair condition. But the rest all withered away with the onset of the drought. There was utter scarcity of drinking water in the western parts of the Zamindari. There was a cloudy sky for few days and it raised several hopes among the people. On 29 March evening there was a slight drizzle for few miles to the south of Sankar Royal pet and on 31 March, three miles south-east of Punganur; and nothing else. The free kitchen of Ramasamudram continued to feed 45 people (1 man, 5 women and 39 children). Grain was brought by the traders from Madras and Vellore. It was reported that about 27 tons (316 bags) of rice was brought between 15-31 March 1892. During the fortnight the amount of rice imported rose to 600 bags.

There were about 471 coolies employed on several relief works in the Zamindari like repair of Punganur-Chowdepalle

Road, construction of a new road from Ramasamudram to Cuddapah border and deepening of 11 potable water wells.[19] By the end of April, the number of coolies rose to 594 people. On 16 April the coolies on one government relief work had struck work as the wages were very low.

The supply of water became so scanty that people had to wait a long time before they could fill up their pots. The collection of Peishscush and the additional quit-rent on the Punganur Zamindari amounting to Rs.68,839-8-9 up to April, was postponed by the Government due to drought conditions in the Zamindari. The Government of Madras and the Commissioner, Land Revenue Settlement visited Punganur on 15 May, 1892 and inspected the relief camps and saw the condition of the laborers on such works. By this time, the foot and mouth diseases for the cattle broke out. The Collector wrote in his periodical report:

> Five families were found to be in bad condition at Boduvaripalle, 11 miles to the north of Punganur. They had no stocks of grain in their huts. In three of these houses, the women were seen cooking tamarind seeds for their meal. They were advised to go to the relief works going on near Punganur, but they declined to go so far, pleading various excuses.[20]

There were also few cases of Cholera in Punganur and Kandukur but soon the epidemic abated.

In view of the famine conditions, the Collector recommended to the Board in April, 1892 that the Peishscush on the Zamindar be reduced. But the Board after examination, felt that the Zamindar should cut down his expenses on administration and declined to recommend any reduction in the Pieshcush. The Board further made the policy of the British Government clear when it said:

> The sole big benefit to Government of the Zamindari System is that a revenue of a fixed sum is secured and to give up that benefit is to abandon the principal or one of the principal advantages of the system.[21]

Thus the plea of the Collector to reduce the annual peishcush was turned down. However, the Board felt that in view of the loss of income sustained by the Zamindar, he might be granted three years' time for the payment of his Peishscush.

When the famine became acute, the cart hire has gone up by 50 percent because of the lack of fodder. The ryots had to strive every nerve to preserve the working cattle by digging up for grass roots. About the condition of cattle all over the Zamindari, the fortnightly report ending 31 May 1892 says:

> The cattle suffer greatly. The majority of them can only get one drink a day though twice a day would not be too many in this hot weather. Effort is made to improve the water supply in places which are badly off. The stall fed cattle are better. The rest in the affected parts are generally getting thin and emaciated. It is noticed that of the cattle in a herd or even belonging to the same individual, some are in a tolerably fair condition, while some are markedly emaciated. To add to the misery of the latter, they are sometimes mercilessly pecked by crows when no one is near to drive them away. The ghastly sores, one sees now and then, on the backs of some of these animals are, indeed frightful.[22]

The Special Deputy Collector noticed that during the month of May there was death of 25 head of cattle of which 13 were cows, 1 bullock, 7 calves and 4 she-buffaloes. It was also reported that in Punganur town, Sadum, Kandur and Kothakota there were 15 deaths due to Cholera. There was a steady increase of laborers at the relief camps. At road construction and clearing of wells, the number of laborers rose from 549 on 30 April to 1357 on 14 May and again to 1862 on 28 May, 1892.[23]

On 29 May a disastrous fire occurred in the village, Kamminagari Palle, 6 miles from Punganur and destroyed 82 out of 96 houses in that village. There was great loss of property. Food grains stored in all these houses were destroyed. About 4 head of cattle got burnt. It was estimated by the Special Deputy Collector that there was a loss of more than 3 thousand Rupees. Later, the ryots of the village were granted by the Zamindar free licenses for building materials.[24]

By the beginning of June, the season started to show signs of improvement in Punganur. On the night of 2 June 1892, there was a fall of 1.70 inches of rain and this has revived hope in the people. There was fair rainfall during the next few weeks and with that the grass started sprouting up and pasture started to improve. Owing to the demand for ploughing, there was a sharp rise in the price of cattle fit for work. However, the Cholera at Punganur, Kandur, Kilapatla and Gangivari palle went unabated and about 48 deaths were reported from all these places. Due to the Cholera scare, the number of coolies went down at relief camps. The Board of Revenue instructed the Collector that the wages at the relief works should be reduced to "second class wage" as there was rainfall in the Zamindari and that the work under tanks were to absorb labour.[25]

By June end the standing crops improved as there was a rainfall of 6.6 inches in the fortnight ending 30 June. There was pasture and fodder available in sufficient quantity. As the recent rains have greatly improved the stock of the Zamindari, the relief camp was at once closed down by the Government. But the Special Deputy Collector wrote to the Board requesting that he be allowed to carry the relief work till 15 July and this was approved by a Telegram to him.[26] Accordingly all relief works were closed in the Zamindari. The Special Deputy Collector who was deputed to supervise all relief works was withdrawn.[27]

The months of June and July 1892 were quite propitious for Punganur. During these months there was good rainfall when compared to the same period during the earlier 4 year period. The rainfall was as follows:

Table 8-4: Rainfall for June & July (1888-1892)

Month	*1888*	*1889*	*1890*	*1891*	*1892*
June	1.00	3.30	2.60	1.78	9.40
July	1.05	3.30	2.05	1.40	5.05

Source: Rainfall statistics in Report of the season in Punganur Zamindari for the month of July 1892 in BOR, Revenue Settlement Land Records and Agriculture (RSLRA), 10 August 1892 No. 559.

The tanks have all received fair supply and wet cultivation also started. But the supply in the tanks was not uniform due to local variations in the rainfall. The tanks in the following places have received good supply of water sufficient for the paddy crop. The places were:

Sankar Royalpet	Peddakurapalle
Gunderkul	Ulapadu
Kilakeri	Muthukur
Vanewaladinne	Chalamangalam
Yalava Nellore	Kilapatla
Ramasamudram	Avulapalle
Chembakur	Nanjampet
Nariganipalle[28]	

The rain in the western parts of the Zamindari was heavier than in the eastern parts. The tanks between Punganur and the hills to the east had the smallest supply. There was an extent of 25,000 acres of dry land which had crops like *Ragi, Cumbu,*

Cholam, *Machai, Dhall, Samai* and *Vargu (*all millets). The Special Deputy Collector, R. Sunder Row on his return from Punganur Zamindari to Vellore, district headquarters, reported that "the prospects in the Zamindari are good and a few showers in the course of a fortnight will remove all apprehensions."[29] The position of drinking water improved and the condition of the cattle improved. Public health also improved as there were no Cholera cases. Prices of grain also slightly fell when compared to earlier months. Importing of foodgrains by inhabitants from Vellore and Madras also came down on account of the favorable turn of the season. Yet the Government felt the need to repair Punganur- Sankar Royal Pet road and the Chembakur road for purposes of easy communication facilities.

At the time when relief operations were closed, there were about 47 loan applications pending and the amount involved was Rs.6730. But owing to the change with season, applicants in many cases, did not press for the grant of loans.

With the signs of the famine abating, the Board also was not in favor of conceding the requests of the Zamindar for reduction of the Peishscush nor for remission of the amount that was due to be paid as arrears of peishcush.[30] However the Board suggested that the Zamindar should cut down his expenditure so that he will be able to pay his peishcush without much difficulty. Yet the Collector felt that the Zamindar should be exempted from the payment of any interest on the installments he was due.

The Zamindar Shankar Royal who earlier had applied for permission of the Government to lay a Telephone line from his Palace to his garden as early as 1890 has put aside the plan because of the impending bad season in his Zamindari.[31] The Board took up the matter in early October and instructed the Collector to find out whether the Zamindar was willing to have such a

Telephone line opened and maintained by the Government Telephones Department.[32]

After the 1892 famine, there was again an acute season in 1896. Punganur and the northern part of Palamaner suffered most in the entire North Arcot District. In Punganur there was a sudden heavy rise in prices in the third week of October, 1896. In September the rainfall was less than all other places. The Collector on knowing of the sudden rise in prices of food grains, sent the Divisional Officer to make a tour of Punganur and report. The officer reported that the sudden rise in prices of grain was due to the influx of people at Punganur for the Dasarah. But the Divisional Officer's report spoke about the seriousness of things especially in the portions bordering Mysore and Cuddapah districts where most of the crops were dry. The Ragi crop on which the people chiefly depended was found to be almost lost. Regarding the rainfall, the Divisional Officer reported that Punganur recorded a rainfall of 6.79 inches for the period from June to August, 1896 whereas the average for the above period was 9.02 inches. For September, 1896 the rainfall was 3.45 inches; when the average stood at 3.68 inches. For the month of October, 1896 there was rainfall of only 1.46 inches while the average was to the extent of 6.37 inches.[33] The Deputy Collector found that there was good deal of demand for work. The wages in the Zamindari were slightly higher in other places on the plateau because of the demand for labour at the Kolar Gold mines.

The condition of the cattle in Punganur became precarious due to failure of rains, and this was seen in the rise of the number of such cattle brought for sale at slaughter houses.[34] By December, 1896, the situation still deteriorated. The area near Tsudupalle was better in the Zamindari where the dry crop did not fail. But the central portion of the Zamindari suffered badly. The tanks became empty and the state of Ragi crop in many parts became hopeless. Around Somala the appearance of the Ragi crop was very pathetic. The Deputy Collector who toured that area reported that "the Ragi crop to all appearance is absolutely dead and dry. If a match had been applied to it, the whole crop would have blazed for miles".[35]

The Collector visited nearly 43 villages in the entire Zamindari and reported to the Board of Revenue on the conditions of the people. He felt that a large number of people were ready to come for the *famine wages* if the work was in their own villages, but they would not go elsewhere. He also wrote that in the western part of the Zamindari "relief may become necessary in the future, but I do not think necessity has yet arisen. It will require careful watching and I have already given orders to this effect.[36]

The situation slightly improved by early 1897 when the crops have not only sprouted again, but have grown luxuriously. It was high and thick and from a distance, the ears of the Ragi crop appeared large and full. When the Collector was still in town, there was good rain and he felt that there was more hope at the end of the tour than at the beginning.[37]

A common feature of the ryots was to sell land. Land was bought by well to do persons as a sort of investment and also because sometimes it had a price lower than its usual worth. There were also cases of migrations from Thattupalle village to far off Natal. The reason was that they could not eke out a living at their place. Thettupalle had several iron smelting ovens and bully made iron was used for making ploughs. But these ovens went into disuse with the coming of the iron-plough in the market.[38]

By 1897 January, there was drought in Zamindari. The Collector S.H. Wynne reported that Ragi crop which came into ears after the rains in November (1896) and grew well has turned to be poor and there were no hope of getting even a 4 anna crop. Drinking water was insufficient in many villages. Though cattle were not dying, fodder became insufficient.[39] The Collector then ordered the Deputy Collector to tour the affected parts of Punganur Zamindari where some people were reported to be eating *Gottigaddelu* and *aloe* roots. The officer toured the Zamindari for 5 days from 2 to 7 February, 1897 and reported that the poorer sections had supplies of Ragi and other pulses and "they were more busy and cheerful than I found them at my last inspection."[40] The Board in its periodical review also felt that the entire district was fairly better except Punganur.[41] By December, 1897 there were good rains all over the Zamindari and the tanks were all full even before the North-east monsoon had set in. The ryots started to let out water from the tanks as they were afraid of breaches.[42]

At the turn of the century, even in 1901 there were utter scarcity conditions in February-March. The Acting Collector, R.H. Campbell writing to the Commissioner of Revenue on 28 March, 1901 stated that "continued high prices, and a prolonged agricultural depression have nearly exhausted the resources of the bulk of the ryots population and dried up the sources of private charity. Beggars have been congregating in large towns".[43] The Collector also pointed out that there was migration to Natal and Mauritius and also unregistered migration to Kolar Gold Fields in very large number.[44]

A Punganur Migrant in S.A

During the famines of 1891-92, migrations from Punganur Zamindari to far off places like Natal, (South Africa), Penang, Singapore, Burma and Fiji were reported. One such was from Nellimanda village, about 25 km. from Punganur, where a 27 year old Ramaiah Naidu migrated as an indentured laborer to Natal during the 1901 famine never to return but made it big later in life. His story was completely forgotten till about a century, when a grand-daughter of Ramaiah Naidu, after frantic efforts by plowing through the shipping records of 1900s at the Archival repositories at Johannesburg and other places, was able to trace the trail of his migration from Nellimanda to Natal. Finally, she made a successful trip to Nellimanda in 2015 and visited the ancestral village of her grandfather.

Her visit to Nellimanda in search of her roots and meeting the family, which must be of her grandfather's, if only he has not left a century and quarter ago, was the result of her sheer courage of conviction and determination to establish her family links to the village that Ramaiah Naidu left just to escape the wrath of the famine and in search of a living.

The Hindu published an article, "From Africa With Love", by the present author, on the visit of Ms. Sharmini Naidoo, the grand- daughter of Ramaiah Naidoo to Nellimanda in Punganur, in its Friday Review columns, dated, 17 July, 2015. The excerpts of the article are reproduced here as it is self explanatory.

Nellimanda, a small village having about 50 households and having a population of less than 300, is 25 Km north east of Punganur, in the present day Chittoor District of Andhra Pradesh. A month ago the entire village folk in Nellimanda was elated with the arrival of a foreign guest to the house of Venkataramana. A lady in her 40s, in her Jeans and a T, the color and texture of which was clearly not familiar to the locals, came visiting the family which she could have called her grand-father, Ramaiah Naidu's home had he not left it a century ago.[45]

Ramiah's name itself has slipped away from the collective memory of the family and the village except some seniors of the village vaguely remembering their elders saying that someone from Venkataramana's house has gone to *Natalam*, a far off place on the other side of the deep seas'.

As she got down the taxi at Venkataramana's modest house, gaudily painted, with a posy of cows, buffalos and few sheep tied up in the front yard, accompanied by a Telugu knowing Travel agent, she could imagine the long and arduous journey her grand-father made. In spite of the language barriers, she mingled well with the women folk of family and neighbors, took photographs, videographed the surroundings, noted down their names of all the family members, the now branched up and the extended families in the village, their relationships much to the delight of all the villagers. After spending several hours, she took leave of her long lost and now discovered, 'cousins' particularly Venkataramana and their respective spouses.

Punganur was a major Zamindari in Andhra (then in Madras presidency) for centuries before Indian independence. The Zamindari suffered from several devastating famines throughout the 19th Century. Around 1900 it became common for the villagers in the Punganur Zamindari to migrate to far off places in search of a living.

South Africa, known in those days as Natal, was the most favored destination for migrations, though Kolar Gold Fields (KGF) was a big attraction. There were cases of migration to other British colonies like Penang, Singapore, Burma and Fiji, as well. Abject poverty, lack of agricultural works and the absence of institutional succor were the common push factors for the migrations. There were also the pull factors like the promise of the agents a hassle free life in the new colonies, the wild imagination that the streets there are paved with gold and the houses are studded with diamonds; and above all the utopian thought of adventure to explore, risking for an unknown world to make a fortune, were common among the village young with less encumbrances.

Young Ramaiah Naidu,[46] with contacts established through an agent, probably left with no more than a pair of clothes. Life as indentured labour in the fields of British planters in South Africa could not have been easy for Ramaiah. But once he got freed himself of indenture contract, Ramaiah's fortunes gradually changed for the better. Working hard with odd jobs, he became popular and respected among his fellow south Indian settlers. Over years, he got married to the daughter of a fellow Tamil worker and settled down there, forgetting his place of birth, Nellimanda near Punganur.

Ramaiah educated all his children well, as he knew what it was for him without proper education. During his later years, Ramaiah used to narrate tales of Nellimanda, the village he grew up in far away South India, to his sons and their families. But as Ramaiah's descendants were busy with their own lives, they never thought they could establish their lost links with Nellimanda. But a grand-daughter of Ramaiah Naidu (by then he was Naidoo, as the settlers of that community preferred to style themselves), Sharmini Naidoo, who was a CEO of a Cargo transport Company, always longed to see Nellimanda, where the protagonist, her grand- father was born and brought up.

While browsing through books in the Library at the University of Cape Town, where her brother is a Dean, Shirmini Naidoo came across an article on " Famines and Famine Relief Measures in Punganur Zamindari: 1800-1948" in a journal ICFAI, published from Hyderabad. Punganur, was a familiar word that used to crop up often in the family discussions, and Nellimanda, she knew, was connected with Punganur. She immediately contacted the author of the article, a professor of History at the University of Hyderabad, whose mail I.D. was provided with the article itself. As per his guidance, she started perusing the relevant Archival records at Johannesburg. After a protracted and rigorous search, she found an entry in the shipping records that "Ramaiah, 27, of Nellimanda in the Thana of Punganur,"[47] did leave Madras to Natal in 1901. She even got the name of the Steamer, S.S. Congella that carried the passengers with the details of other sailors and also the name of the British planter to whom Ramaiah was indentured. Ramaiah's migration was now a historical reality established by her effort and research. Till then Ramaiah's narrative was bordering on myth and belief for the family.[48]

Shirmini flew down to Chennai (it was Madras when Ramaiah Naidu left) and with the help of her travel agency, took a cab and travelled 250 km North-west to reach Nellimanda in order to fulfill her cherished desire to see the place and establish links with her cousins and their families. With no one in Nellimanda known or familiar, her visit all the way from a metropolis in South Africa to that small village near Punganur in remote Chittoor district of Andhra Pradesh was like an adventure tale directly from a fantasy movie and a dream come true. She is immensely happy for her family is not devoid of its roots. They are strongly entrenched in Nellimanda. And she even visited it.

"The effort and expense incurred, and the time spent in my search for records is nothing before the gratification that now I have, My family is not from nowhere, but from Nellimanda. Had I not by chance read that article about the famines in Punganur by the Hyderabad based Professor K.S.S. Seshan, I cannot imagine to have succeeded in getting to know of my ancestral roots in far off Nellimanda in far away South India" Shirmini Naidoo gratefully acknowledges.

A Note from South Africa

(*A granddaughter remembers the story of the Punganur migrant, Ramaiah Naidu, who made big in South Africa)*

As a young girl playing under the coconut palms at my father's family home (which was built by my grandfather), I would often gaze at the portrait of my paternal grandfather Mr Ramiah Naidoo. As I grew older, I felt a growing need to find out more about him. I admired the fact that even during the harsh times of the British rule in South Africa he was still able to give the family so much and have always felt that he should be acknowledged for his incredible endeavours.

Thanks to Professor KSS Seshan's wonderful gesture I am now able to share my grandfather's story. I first came across Professor Seshan's article on the famine in Arcot whilst trying to find my grandfather's family in Nellimanda after 120 years. He was kind enough to reply to a mail to assist me in trying to find my family and even assisted me in planning my visit to my grandfather's village. Professor Seshan has maintained regular correspondence with me over the past nine years and has shared the rich history and heritage of Nellimanda and Punganur which I am extremely grateful for and makes me feel so proud to be a second generation Indian.

Below is the story of my grandfather, Ramiah Naidoo who despite the hardship and adversities in his life is considered to be one of the many successes of the indentured labourers in Natal, South Africa

Deceived like many Indians by the British Empire about the land that promised riches and gold my grandfather decided at the age of 27 years to leave his family in Nellimanda and his beloved India in the hope of earning a better living in a foreign land.

From 1860 to the early 1900's, the British Empire created an opportunity for "escape" to places like the colony of Natal in South Africa. Many Indians were lured with false promises and dreams of a better life in this new land. Some were defrauded into migrating whilst others chose to make a new start in South Africa.

During this time, the Indians in South Africa were exposed to harsh and oppressive conditions, with their only value being perceived in the labour that they had to sell on the white market to boost the economy. Indians were also derogatively referred to as "coolies" to denote their lowly status. Whilst a few prospered others lived in abject poverty or simply endured the hardship of indenture. Most Indians were not even allowed to bring their wives and minor children to the country.

Unknown to him, my grandfather was also brought into the country as an indentured labourer, which was really nothing more than a common slave.

He travelled by ship to South Africa aboard the SS Congella and arrived in Durban, Port Natal on 26 October 1901. There are many documented stories on the treacherous conditions that the Indians had to endure on these journeys to South Africa and I fear that my grandfather also suffered these hardships.

Upon arrival in Durban my grandfather was indentured to Mr William Gray, a landowner in Springfield, Durban. He had to work for five years, six days a week and nine hours per day. He was paid a lowly pittance of a wage for working these long hours from Monday to Saturday in the harsh South African climate. He was given a basic ration of rice, dhall, salt fish, oil or ghee and salt for the month. It is difficult to visualise how my grandfather and the other indentured labourers survived with such a paltry wage and so few provisions. But despite the struggle his dogged willpower and determination allowed him to save sufficient money and after five hard years he was able to buy his "freedom" as a free Indian. This was an amazing feat at the time as many of the indentured Indians were unable to afford their freedom.

After attaining his freedom my grandfather decided not to return to India but rather to pursue his dream of earning a successful living so that he could support his family in India. With the knowledge and experience acquired in farming he boldly ventured out on his own. My grandfather followed his life- long passion - farming and independence. He moved to the outskirts of Tongaat to a place called Herrwood - some 40 km north of Durban where he leased a small plot and engaged in banana farming. Years later my father would learn from one of my grandfather's peers about my grandfather's great skill at growing big bananas.

Like all small farmers in those days, my grandfather also owned a couple of cows, a few goats, and some fowl. Sundays and public holidays were happy occasions. A rooster or hen provided for a good meal for family and friends.

When his banana farm prospered, he was astute enough to invest in agricultural property in and around Tongaat. Tongaat is a small coastal town that was developed as a result of its vast sugar cane fields. The town is home to the oldest Indian community in South Africa, having been where the first indentured Indian labourers were brought to work in the sugar-cane plantations.

By 1927 my grandfather sold all his small holdings and bought a sugar cane farm of twenty-five acres. This was to be his permanent residence until his demise on 20 July 1947.

When my grandfather moved to his new farm, he built a wood and iron building to accommodate his growing family. It is indeed amazing that with an agricultural background he had so much talent and was so very progressive and ingenious for his time. By 1939 he had enough of leaking roofs and mud floors and decided to build his dream house. He manufactured his own building blocks and built a six- bedroom house with huge verandas, a free- standing kitchen, pantry, and bathroom. (Many Indians lived in tin houses at the time) With the lack of running water in the village he built a deep underground well (tank) to store rainwater. Shortly thereafter he also bought a general dealers shop in the village centre.

Life on the farm was arduous. My grandfather worked tirelessly on the farm from sunrise to sunset. Many a time the family assisted in planting the sugar cane. Like most individual farmers he had his own plough and mules to dig the furrows during the planting season. Harvesting the cane was done by private contractors. The crop was sold to the local sugar mill and payment was made in instalments.

To augment his income, he planted cash crops such as peas, beans, rice, nuts and avocados. Fruit such as mandarins, oranges, guavas, china guavas, shaddocks, jackfruits, litchis, mangoes, and bananas were also planted around the house. Like all farmers my grandfather also had a few cows to provide the family with fresh milk daily. Even the milking of the cows was done by him.

Meals were basic and cooked in open fire and later on coal stoves. Lunch consisted of dhall, beans, jackfruit and other seasonal garden vegetables with mealie rice or roti (chapati and paratha). Rice was a scarce commodity. Supper was mainly Sangati (stiff mealie meal porridge) with left over curries. On some weekends, a chicken could be spared for a curry. Mutton was a delicacy and fish was seldomly eaten. During the weekends mealie meal porridge and pickle was breakfast. Due to my grandfather's resourcefulness he was able to provide a better life for his family than most of the other Indian families at the time.

Although my grandfather was far away from his motherland, he did not forget his mother tongue and customs. He conversed only in Telugu to his family and friends and continued to read and write in the vernacular. All his financial records were in Telugu. I am fortunate enough to still have his account book in my possession which is also in Telugu.

My grandfather ensured that the family continued with the customs, prayers, and festivals that the indentured brought to Natal.Festivals like Deepavali, Porridge prayers, Pongal, Purtassi and Kavady were observed and are still celebrated by the remaining family. Rituals during weddings, funerals and other occasions were also followed as in Nellimanda and in other parts of South India.

After my grandfather's demise my grandmother and my father's eldest brother (who had to leave school to run the farm) tried to sustain the farming activities but after a while with the scarcity of capital, manpower and my grandfather's expertise, the sugar cane farming eventually ceased. Some of the land was given to the family and they lived in close proximity to each other. My parents still reside near the old family house which has now been demolished.

This was such a blessing to have been given land at a time when land acquisition was very costly and almost inaccessible to Indians (as a result of the racial segregation and limited job opportunities for Indians during the apartheid era). The remaining land was later developed into a new residential township. The main road leading into the township is named after my grandfather – and is known as Ramiah Drive. And another street is named after my maternal grandmother Kanagamah and is known Kanagamah Road. This at least provides some recognition to the man that endured many hardships and left a legacy behind.

My grandfather raised thirteen children, (he was married twice as his first wife passed away early) seven daughters and six sons. Unfortunately, none of the sons took to farming. Two sons ventured into commerce and four sons into the education sector as teachers. The daughters married and raised their own families. The thirty-eight grandchildren (my cousins) have all achieved success in their respective chosen fields of vocation and I hope that our achievements and our continued family traditions and values would have made my grandfather very proud.

Whilst in South Africa, my grandfather continued to maintain contact with his family in India and used to regularly write and send monies to them. However, after his demise the family lost contact with the Nellimanda family.

The urge to find out more about my grandfather and my roots prompted me to locate the shipping records and gather as much information as I could about him and I eventually decided to visit his village. In 2011, after a long trip from Chennai via NN Kandagai, to make contact with of my grandfather's nieces relatives (her great grandson graciously left his sugar plantation and agreed to come with us to translate) I was finally able to visit Nellimanda. As we neared the village, I saw the palm trees and crops which reminded me so much of Herrwood in Tongaat and in that moment I knew that it had to be my grandfather's village.

The villagers of Nellimanda were so welcoming and warm and treated me like family.

The older women marvelled at my western clothing and the way that I wore my hair.

As I walked around the village we visited the local temple, I saw a villager frying vadas which is a delicacy in South Africa and I also saw a cow which reminded me of the stories about my grandfather and his cows.

It is worth mentioning that I do not speak Telugu but I spoke in English to our travel guide's driver who translated in Tamil (because the driver couldn't speak Telugu) to my relative NN Kandagai who then translated my words into Telugu and even though the whole conversation went back and forth like this in this manner we were still able to understand each other and to this day I still have such fond and heart- warming memories of Nellimanda.

Even though I was unable to find any immediate family living in Nellimanda because I do not know the family name except that my grandfather was of Balija caste, the mayor, Mr Reddy was able to confirm from the land records that my grandfather did indeed live in the village. I am also in contact with one of the young people from the village via social media who is also trying to help me find more information about my grandfather. One of the things that I know about my grandfather is that he was very tall and I gather from him that this is also the trait of the villagers so this is yet another thing that confirms that this is my grandfather's home.

As I write this, I am saddened that my grandfather was unable to go back to his precious India and see his family but I feel so honoured and touched that I was able to visit Nellimanda and hope to take my father to visit soon.

– **Ms. Sharmini Naidoo**
Founder, "A Step Ahead"
Johannesburg
South Africa

Notes

1. This was very much a general condition in most parts of Western India at that time. The information on these later famines of 19th Century was collected "as a part of administration efforts to prevent any given crop failure from leading to high mortality and disruption of agricultural system." Michelle Burge Mc Alpine, Death Famine and Risk in Western India- 1870-1920", in *Journal of Economic History,* Vol. XXXIX, No.1, March, 1979, p. 144.
2. BOR, 2 May 1891, No. 3029.

3. Le Fanu to BOR, Proceedings of the BOR, 18 December, 1891, no. 817.
4. Letter from W.J. Le Fanu, Collector of North Arcot to the Secretary of the Commissioner of Land Revenue Settlement, 19 November, 1891 in BOR, 2 December, 1891.
5. *Ibid.,* 11 December, 1891, BOR No. 817.
6. Letter from W.J.H. Le Fanu Collector of North Arcot, to See Revenue Settlement, 11 December, 1891 in BOR No. 817.
7. Letter from Le Fanu, 3 December 1891 in BOR, 9 December, 1891, No. 784. The rain gauge station in Punganur was set up in 1873. In Madanapalle and Vayalpad also such stations were set up in the same year.
8. *Ibid.*
9. R.D. No. A 813 of 1892, R.O.S.A.T.
10. BOR, 22 January, 1892, No. 47.
11. G.O. 396, 11 February, 1892, State of the season, Report of the Collector, Retain Disposal (R.D. hereafter), 5 February, 1892, No. 813.
12. Le Fanu to Commissioner of Revenue Settlement 1 February, 1892, No. 242 in BOR, 10 February, 1892, No. 92.
13. G.O. 22 February, 1892, Mis. No. 1050 (R)
14. BOR, 25 March, 1892, No. 240.
15. BOR, 14 March, 1892, No. 191.
16. Fortnightly narration of the Punganur Division by the Special Deputy Collector, North Arcot, 16 March 1892, BOR, 22 March, 1892, No. 227.
17. BOR 22 March, 1892, No. 227.
18. BOR Resolution, 16 April, 1892, No. 291.
19. Fortnightly report of the Special Deputy Collector, 1 April, 1892, BOR, 16 April, No. 291.
20. Fortnightly Report of Punganur Division for the period ending 15 May, 1892 from Special Deputy Collector, 16 May, 1892 in BORP, 20 May, 1892, No. 376.
21. BORP, 3 June, 1892, No. 244.
22. Report of the Special Deputy Collector, 1 June, 1892, Camp. Ramasamudram No. 3506 in BORP, 13 June, 1892, No. 423.

23. BOR, *Ibid.,* No. 423.
24. *Ibid.,* No. 423.
25. BORP, 22 June, 1892, No. 451.
26. BOR, 19 July, 1892, No. 519.
27. Government Report (Revenue Settlement) No. 6875, Collector North Arcot, 31 July, 1892, No. 3856.
28. *Ibid.*
29. *Ibid.*
30. G.O. (Revenue Department) 19 July, 1892, No. 737, in BOR 20 August, 1892, No. 454.
31. BOR 5 September, 1892, No. 5600.
32. BOR (Miscellaneous), 18 October, 1892, No. 6667.
33. S.H. Wynne Collector, North Arcot, to the Secretary, Commissioner, of RSLRA, 12 November, 1896, No. 2830, in BOR 19 November, 1896, No. 360.
34. *Ibid.*
35. BOR, 19 December, 1896, No. 452.
36. *Ibid.,* No.452.
37. *Ibid.*
38. Chandrasekhar, *Thettupalle,* p. 102.
39. Collector, North Arcot, to BOR, 17 January, 1897 in BOR, 25 January, 1897, No. 54.
40. BOR, 25 February, 1897, No. 156.
41. BOR, Seasons Report for the week ending 20 February, 1897 in BOR, 23 February, 1897, No. 152.
42. Letter from S.H. Wynne to the Commissioner, dated 14 December, 1896 in BOR, 10 January 1898, No. 9.
43. BORP, 10 April, 1901, No. 58.
44. *Ibid,* No. 58.
45. K.S.S. Seshan, "From Africa With Love", in Friday Review, *The Hindu*, Chennai, July 17, 2015, p. 4.
46. While the shipping records indicate his name as Ramaiah Naidu, in South Africa, his name was spelt as Naidoo; which became the suffix for all his progeny. In 1925 in a discharge document that was obtained for his employer, dated 25 June, 1925, Ramaiah has signed

as Ramaiah Chetty. As Ramaiah's caste was Balija, he could have either Naidu or Chetty as suffix to his name.

47. Thana was the Police Station. Nellimanda then came under the Punganur Police Station. In the Shipping records as well as in the records pertaining to the disembarking, his name, age, name of the village of birth and the Police station alone are given. The absence of any column for surname, make the tracing of the family roots of such migrant, a major problem.

48. Ramaiah seems to have gone through few more contracts of lesser duration after his first long term contract was over. In 1925 there was a discharge form obtained from an employer which suggests that he was indentured to him for thirteen months. Probably that must be the last contract he served as a contract labor before becoming a free man. The text of this Discharge form obtained from D. Sather Bhujan was as follows:: "I D. Sather Bhujan, do hereby leave all liabilities which were agreed verbally between you(Ramaiah Chetty) and I some thirteen months ago. I solemnly declare that I have no more further claims against you from this day of June, 1925,"

Sd.(on a stamped paper) Sather Bhujan,

The three witnesses signed were: 1. C.R. Moonsamy, 2. P.V. Naidoo and 3. Ram Prakash

It is to be seen that Ramaiah Naidoo in this discharge form has signed as Chetty and not as Naidoo, as Balija community people are known as either Naidu or Chetty.

IX

Conclusions

Punganur Zamindari, for a very long period before the advent of the British, was the seat of a powerful Palem. Its chiefs were not independent rulers but were subordinate to the successive Hindu and Muslim suzerains to whom they paid tribute. Though with caution and circumspection the Palegars supported Hyder Ali, their relations were strained during the period of Tipu Sultan who made an armed attack on Punganur, enhanced the annual peishcush and on non-payment of it even expelled the Palegar for a while. These measures drove the Palegar on to the side of the British during the last Mysore war (1799). Punganur was the only Palem in the entire Ceded Districts that was retained by the British and later elevated to the status of a Zamindari.

Geographically, Punganur being a buffer region between Mysore on one side and Arcot on the other, possessed many strategic mountain passes which opened up into Mysore territory. Because of its sensitive location, British followed a 'wait and see' policy without taking any hasty action in annexing it after the conclusion of the Forth Mysore War. The Zamindari comprised of about 675 revenue villages and extended over 648 square miles. Poor soils, lack of permanent irrigational sources, unfavorable monsoons and lack of adequate transport and communication facilities have all left the Zamindari, a backward region even in terms of the Ceded districts.

Thomas Munro, a great champion of Ryotwari Settlement was responsible for the transfer of the entire Punganur, in stages, to the British, attempted at dispossessing the Palem as he did with regard to all other such Palems in the entire Ceded Districts. But the government with a view not to reduce the entire region to a dumb uniformity and in consideration of the loyalty of the Palegar, decided on its continuation. The period from 1799 to 1861 was a period of experimentation in Punganur with numerous periodical land revenue settlements. The mode of revenue settlements generally affects the condition of the people whose avocation largely rests with agriculture. The annual Peihscush that was collected by the government from the Zamindar was considerably heavy. The frequent requests through memorials, the Zamindars made for the reduction of such heavy annual peishcush were not heeded by the government. This in turn to a large extent contributed to the heavy land rents that the peasants were made to pay to the Zamindar. The unfavorable Tenural structures, coupled with heavy land rents resulted in the tardy growth of agriculture.

Agricultural practices in the Zamindari were marked with tradition and superstition. There were no attempts to introduce commercial crops which must have brought increased returns to the peasants. The frequent crop failures due to drought brought the small and marginal farmers into the ranks of land-less wage earners. These were the classes of the people who were first affected when famines or scarcities occurred. Punganur had several devastating famines during the entire 19th century.

Whenever there was a famine in any part of the Ceded districts, it had its echo in Punganur without exception. The earliest reference to the famines in Punganur was made by Robert

Ross, the Collector of Cuddapah, at the turn of the 19th century. A large number of Punganur peasants were forced to abandon their lands without paying rents due to crop failure. Ten years later when similar famines prevailed, the government showed certain concessions to the Zamindar and he was asked to pay the annual peishcush in a progressive manner. The crop failure was a general cause for the distress during every famine in the Zamindari. One common feature during the famines in Punganur was the steep rise of the price of food grains. Even when convinced of the reduction of the fortunes of the Zamindari, the rigidity of the Permanent settlement was such that the government blatantly refused to reduce the peishcush amount.

The Great Famine which occurred during 1876-78 was the most devastating one in the Zamindari. Locally it was known as *Pedda Karuvu.* A year before this famine, there were heavy rains when many tanks breached in the entire Zamindari. As a severe drought followed the floods, the people greatly suffered. The starving people during this famine ate leaves and roots to keep their bodies and souls together. Starvation deaths became very common. Sadum area in the Zamindari was the most hit during the Great Famine.

The famine of 1891-92 has much information on record because of the preparation of the fortnightly reports by the special deputy collectors of the area. During this famine, Ramasamudram division in the Zamindari suffered most. The cattle died in large numbers due to lack of water and fodder.

The famine relief measures adopted during the famines of the 19th century in the Zamindari make an interesting reading. While in the early phase, there were no serious attempts on the part of the government or on the part of the Zamindar to provide any succor. But after 1880 when the Famine Commission came into being, we observe perceptible change in the relief mobilization. After the Great Famine, the relief provided to the people in the Zamindari came under three broad heads- 1. Relief provided by the Zamindar, 2. Government relief works and 3. Concessions given to the Zamindar by the government.

The Zamindar generally postponed the collection of the revenue from the people whenever there was the occurrence of scarcity or famine. He also opened Langer khanas or poor homes to provide cooked food and shelter to the famine victims. There were occasions when he sought and took loans from the government to provide relief to the peasants. He also undertook works like desilting of the tanks, digging of wells, repairing of tank bunds etc. During the Great famine, Sir Richard Temple, the Governor of Bengal, who visited the Zamindari also spoke about the concern shown by the Zamindar towards the peasants.

The Government relief works were related mostly to laying of the roads, poor feeding, gratuitous relief and grass-cutting. Poor peasants were also encouraged to cultivate cucumbers etc, on the tank bed lands without paying the usual rent. Whenever road works were taken up, there was unprecedented rush for work by the poor peasants. The wages were very low and they were meant to be kept as unattractive as possible. Though a railway line was suggested in the Zamindari as a famine relief work in 1892, it was not taken up by the government as it was found to be uneconomical in the long run. During the famines, the condition of the people in the Zamindari was so acute that the government was made to give the Zamindar certain concessions which otherwise were not granted to any other Zamindar in the Presidency.

Among the main causes for the frequent famines in the Zamindari were the failure of rainfall, the low economic condition of the peasants, unusual rise in prices the absence of any balance in the production of food grains and commercial products etc. There was total absence of the cash crops or the orchards like the mango, coconut or citrus, which were of later phenomenon. Sometimes famines devolved notwithstanding the mere failure of rains. There were occasions when too heavy rains and breaching of tanks also brought the agricultural operations to a halt. But such exigencies were very rare and it happened only on the eve of the Great Famine of 1876-78.

There was the total absence of monetary support either from the Zamindar or from the government in the form of input subsidies which we hear of these days. Whenever the season failed and the signs of famine appeared, the cultivators were unwilling to take any risks to put more money by taking loans from the local money lenders, with the inevitable consequence of abandoning cultivation for the season. As a result many poor peasants were forced to throng to the government relief works to eke out a living. A unique feature of the Punganur famines was the fodder famine whenever there was the scarcity of food grains due to failure of the rains. It was a huge problem for the peasants to save the lives of agricultural cattle due to lack of fodder and water. With live stocks playing a significant role in the rural economy of the Zamindari, lack of fodder proved havoc for the peasants. Large scale cattle deaths and desertions were reported in the Ramasamudram division of the Zamindari during the Great Famine of 1876-78.

The frequent famines have to a great extent retarted the economic life of the region. Punganur, devoid of any major irrigational projects, endowed with poor soils, undulating hilly terrain, with numerous mountain passes opening towards Mysore, lack of transport facilities, tradition bound cultivation sans any modern methods, nor the use of any improved agricultural implements, the region remained under subsistent economy, and vulnerable to scarcities and famines during the entire 19th century. The famines also made many from Punganur villages to migrate to far off places both within the country like Kolar Gold Fields and far off South Africa, Penang and to Fiji. The migration of Ramaiah Naidu from Nellimanda to South Africa in 1901 as an indentured laborer and made it big there in later years, is a case in point. The visit of his grand -daughter in search of the family roots in 2015 has brought to fore the intensity of famines in Punganur Zamindari under the colonial regime.

The system of indirect rule that was prevalent in the Zamindari, to a large extent was detrimental to the wellbeing of the peasants particularly during the times of famines. With divided authority between the Zamindar on one side and the British government on the other, the relief during the bad seasons was slow, meager and tardy. The bureaucratic delays in the system were responsible for the insufficient relief that came too late and too meager. Though personally the Zamindars were humane and interested in providing relief, they were handicapped by the want of necessary funds. The government which collected peishcush, a lump sum amount annually with no qualms, did not willingly take the responsibility of providing immediate relief to the people. The Zamindar on whom the mantle of the welfare of the ryots rested, was left with very little resources after the peishcush was paid to the government. The government which collected peishcush from the Zamindar, did not show the concern on the sufferings of the peasants. Thus the dual system in the Zamindari set up was also a contributory factor in no small measure to the untold suffering of the poorer sections during the famines in Punganur.

The marked difference in the nature of relief provided by the Zamindar and the relief measures initiated by the government during the famines, also are discernable in the case of Punganur Zamindari. The relief works undertaken by the Zamindars were mostly related to works like tank cleaning, digging of wells and feeding the poor, that reflect his concern for the improvement of agriculture. The government on the contrary, bestowed more attention to factors like road laying, besides providing gratuitous relief and setting up of poor homes indicating its interest in bettering communication facilities and not agricultural growth. Government was more concerned to provide easy access to administrative machinery to penetrate into the hitherto inaccessible interiors of the Zamindari. However, provision of relief by taking up grass cutting in the forest fringes, was a unique feature of the Government's Famine relief in Punganur, that was not known in any other part of the Presidency.

Bibliography

I. Primary Sources

Manuscripts

Board of Revenue Consultations
Circulars from the Zamindar's office (Huzur)
Day Books (Palace Account Books)
District Records, Cuddapah, 1802-1856.
District Records, North Arcot, 1856-1911.
District Records, Chittoor, 1911-1948.
Goshwara Account Books.
Jamabandy (Annual Settlement) Accounts
Kaifeyats.
Khats (Letters of Correspondence)
Manuals of Rules of the Zamindari.
Retained Disposals
Title Deeds of the Khanigi Lands.
Village officers' Account Books.
Visitors Books kept at the palace.
Zamindars' Correspondence.

Printed Documents

1 Official Records;

A Concise history of the Jaghirs and Palayams in the District of North Arcot, 1864- 65, Collector's Office, Chittoor.

Descriptive memoirs of Irrigation works in the Gudiyatham Minor Basin,

Punganur and Bangarupalyam Zamindaries and Madanapalle Taluk, (Madras,1900)

Guide to the Records of North Arcot District, 1800-1835, Collector's Office, Vellore.

Hand-Book to the revenue records of the Ceded Districts, Madras, 1932.

Standing Order of the Board of Revenue,(Land Revenue Settlement and Miscellaneous ,1919, Madras, 1920, in 2 Vols.

The Chittoor District Gazettes 1911-1929, (publication of Official News) Regional Office of the State Archives, Tirupati.

The Fort St. George Gazette, Weekly publication of official News,

1. Official Reports

Benson's Report on the tour of Cuddapah and North Arcot District, 1878-1879, (Madras, 1880).

C.Rundall's Revenue Settlement Report of North Arcot District, 1890.

Annual Reports of on the Administration of the Madras Presidency During the years from 1860-61 to 1938-39.

Report of the Commissioners for the Interrogation of Alleged Cases of Torture in the Madras Presidency, Madras, 1855.

Report on the District plan of Chittoor, by V.S. Sampath, Chittoor Collectorate.

District Census Hand Book: Chittoor District, By T. Vedantam (Ed.), Hyderabad, 1973.

2. *Manuals, Gazettes and Gazetteers*

Boswell, J.A.C. *Manuel of Nellore District*, Madras, 1873.

Brakenbury, C.F. *Madras District Gazetteers, Cuddapah*, Madras, 1915.

Chetty, N. Gopalakrishnama, *A Manual of Kurnool District*, Madras, 1886.

Cox, Arthur.F. *A Manual of the North Arcot District,* Madras, 1881.

Gribble, J.D.B. *A Manual of the District of Cuddapah,* Madras, 1875.

Maclean, C.D. *Manual of the Administration of the Madras Presidency,* Madras, 1885-1893.

Rajagopal, M.V. "Chittoor District Gazetteer" (Draft) AP State Archives, Hyderabad, 1969.

Rice, B. Lewis, *Mysore gazetteer,* Revd. Edition, London, 1897.

Richards, F.J. *Madras District Gazetteers: Salem, Madras, 1918, 2 Vols.*

Sivasankaranarayana, Ch. *Cuddapah District Gazetteer,* Hyderabad, 1967.

Stuart, Harold A. *Madras District Manuals: North Arcot,* Madras, 1895.

II. SECONDARY SOURCES

A. *Books*

Aitchison, C.U. *A Collection of Treaties Engagements and Sunnads,* vol.V, Calcutta, 1864, Vol. IX. Calcutta, 1892.

Anderson, G. *British Administration of India*, London, 1913.

Arbuthnot, A.J. *Selections from the Minutes and other official writings of Major –General Sir Thomas Munro,* Madras, 1886.

Baden –Powell, B.H. *The Land Systems of British India,* London, 1892, 3 Vols.

Balambal,V. *Feudatories of South India, 800-1070 AD.* Allahabad, 1978.

Baliga, B.S. *Studies in Madras Administration*, Madras, 1949.

Bapineedu, Maganti. *Andhra Sarvaswamu,* Rajahmundry, 1961.

Baeglehole, T.H. *Thomas Munro and the development of Administrative Policy in Madras, 1792-1818: the origins of the Munro system,* London, 1966.

Bhatia, B.M. *Famines in India: A study in Some aspects of the Economic History of India,1860-1945,* Bombay, 1963.

Bhattacharyya, S. *Financial Foundations of the British Raj*, Shimla, 1971.

Bradshaw, John. *Sir Thomas Munro and the British Settlement of the Madras Presidency,* London, 1906.

Coleridge,F.A. *A Brief History of Madanapalle*, Trichinopoly, 1911.

Coupland, R. *Britain and India*, London, rpt. 1943.

Digby, William. *Prosperous British India*, rpt. New Delhi, 1969.

Donappa,Thoomati, *Andhra Samsthanamulu Sahithya Poshana*, Tel. Waltair, 1969.

Dube, S.C. *Indian Village*, Bombay, 1967.

Dutt, R.C. *The Economic History of India*, London, 8 th. Ed. London, 1956.

Edwardes, Michael. *Raj: The Story of the British In India*, London, 1967.

Ferminger, Walter, Kelley. *Historical Introduction to the Bengal portion of the Fifth Report,* rpt. Delhi, 1977.

Forrest, Denys. Tiger of Mysore, *The Life and Death of Tipu Sultan*, London, 1970.

Foster, Sir William. *John Company*, London, 1926.

Fraser, R.W. *British India*, London, 1896, rpt. New Delhi, 1974.

Frykenberg, Robert, Eric. Ed. *Land Tenure and Peasant in South Asia*, New Delhi, 1977.

Gleig, G.R. *The Life of Major –General Sir Thomas Munro Late governor of Madras, with extracts from letters and Private Papers,* London, 1830 rpt. 1831.

Gowda, M. Shankar Linge, *Indian Economic Census: Incidence of Land Rent in the Madras* Zamindaries, Madras, 1936.

Gupta ,Sulekha Chandra, *Agrarian Relations and Early British Rule in India*, Bombay, 1963.

Hettne, Bjorn. *The Political Economy of Indirect Rule, Mysore 1881-1947* New Delhi, 1978.

Hiebert, Paul G. *Konderu: Structure and Integration in a South Indian Village,* University of Minnisota, 1971.

Hussain, Yusuf, *The First Nizam: The Life and Times of Nizam-ul- Mulk Asaf Jah* I, rpt. Bombay, 1963.

Iyengar, S. Sundararaja. *Land Tenures in the Madras Presidency, Students' Edition*, Madras, 1933.

Kesavanarayana, B. *Political and Social Factors in Andhra*, Vijayawada, 1976.

Khan, Mohd. Abdul Waheed (ed). *Brief History of Andhra Pradesh*, Hyderabad, 1972.

Kincaid and Parasnis. *A History of the Maratha People*, OUP, 1918-25, 3 Vols.

Kirmani, Mir Hussain Ali *History of Tipu Sultan*, Col. Miles Trans. 1864, 2 nd. Edn. Calcutta, 1958.

Krishnaswami, P.R. Tom *Munro Sahib*, Madras, 1947.

Krishnaswami, S.Y. *Rural Problems in Madras: Monograph*, Madras, 1947.

Kumar, Dharma. *Land and Caste in South India*, CUP, rpt. New Delhi, 1992

Matthai, John. *Village Government in British India*, London, 1931.

Mishra, Girish. *Agrarian Problems of Permanent Settlement: A Case study of Champaran*, New Delhi, 1978.

Mukherjee, Nilmani. *A Bengal Zamindar Jayakrishna Mukherjee of Uttarapara and his Times,* 1808- 1888, Calcutta, 1975.

—————— The Ryotwari System in Madras, 1792- 1827, Calcutta, 1962.

Raghavaingar, Srinivasa. Memorandum on the Progress of the Madras Presidency during the last forty years of British Administration, Madras, 1892.

Rajayyan, K. Administration and Society in the Carnatic, 1701- 1801, Tirupati, 1966.

Raju, Sarada. A. *Economic Conditions in the Madras Presidency, 1800-1850,* Madras, 1941.

Ramaswamy, Kavali, Venkata. *Description of Historical Sketches of Cities and Places in the Deccan*, Calcutta, 1828.

Ranga, N.G. *Economic Conditions of the Zamindari Ryots: The Report of the Enquiry Committee, 1933*, Bezwada, 1933.

—————— *Revolutionary Peasants*, New Delhi, 1949.

Rao, C. Hayavadana, *History of Mysore*, Bangalore, 1946. 3 Vols.

Reddi, Nallapareddi, Chandrasekhara, *Vikrama Simhapuri Mandala Sarvaswamu*, Tel. Nellore, 1963.

Reddi, P.C. The Andhra Pradesh land Reforms, (Ceilings on Agricultural

Holdings), Act. 1973 with a Commentary, Nellore, 1975.

Row, R. Raghoonath, *A brief History of Kalahasti in the Presidency of Madras*, Madras, 1891.

Saheb, Meer Mohammad, *Extracts of Notes by European Travelers in the Books kept at the Palace of H.H. the Rajah Sahib C.I.E. of Punganur*, Madras, 1884.

Sainath.P, *Everybody Loves a Good Drought: Stories from India's Poorest Districts*, New Delhi, 1996, rpt. 2017.

Sampath, M.D. *Chittoor Through the Ages*, Delhi, 1980.

Sarma, Mallampalle Somasekhara, *Vignana Sarvaswamu, Telugu Encyclopaedia*, Madras, 1961.

Sastri, V. Lakshminarasimha, *Encyclopaedia of the Madras Presidency and the Adjacent States*, n.p,n.d.

Sayana, V.V. *The Agrarian Problems of Madras Presidency, Bombay, 1949.*

Sen, Amarthya. *Poverty and Famines, An Essay on Entitlement and Deprivation*, OUP. 1981.

Sen, Sunil. *Agrarian Relations in India*, 1793-1947, New Delhi, 1979.

Seshan, K.S.S. *British Role in Rural Economy, (A Case study of Punganur Zamindari)*, New Delhi, 1989

Sivaswamy, K.G. *Sub-Tenancy in Zamindari Areas*, Madras, 1947.

Slater, Gilbert. *Economic Studies, Some South Indian villages*, London, 1918.

——————— *South India : Its Political and Economic Problems*, London, 1936.

——————*The Dravidian Element in Indian Culture,* New Delhi, rpt. 1976.

—————— Subramanyam, V. *Transplanted Indo-British Administration*, New Delhi, 1977.

Sutherland, J. *Sketches of the Relations subsisting between the British Government in India and the* Different Native states, Calcutta, 1837.

Symons Captain John. *History of Kangundi*, n.d;n.p.

Taylor, Medows. *Tipu Sultan: Abridged and Annotated by Henry Martin*, London,

Thomas, P.J. and . Ramakrishna, K.C., *Some South Indian Villages: A Re survey with Analysis and Observations,* Madras, 1940.

Thomas.P.J. and Sundararama Sastry, *Indian Agricultural Statistics*, Madras, 1940.

Vadivelu, A. The Ruling Chiefs, Nobles and Zamindars of India, Madras, 1915.

Venkataramanaiah, Nelaturi. *Velugotivamsavali*, Tel. Madras, 1938.

Vittal, B.P.R. *Reorganisation of District Administration in AP – A Case Study*, New Delhi, 1968.

Wilson, H.H. *A Glossary of Judicial and Revenue Terms …* London, 1885, Indian Edn. Delhi,1968.

2. Articles in Journals

Anjaneyulu, M.S.R. " Permanent Settlement in the Second Division of the Visakhapatnam District- A Case Study ", *Itihas,* Journal of the AP State Archives, Hyderabad Vol. IV, No. 2. 1976.

Azad, Melampati. "Challapalle Zamindari Bhoomula Akramana Udyamamu" *Visalandhra,* Tel. Vijayawada, Vol. 29, No. 106, 12 September, 1979.

Dua, J.C. " Poligars : Their Rise in the Ceded Districts" *Proceedings of the Indian History Congress*, 33rd. Session, 1972.

Mc Alpine, Michelle Burge, "Death, Famine and Risk: The Changing impact of Crop failures in Western India, 1870-1920" *Journal of Economic History (J.E.H.)* Vol. XXXIX, No.1, March, 1979.

McLane, John R."Peasants, Money lenders and Nationalists at the end of the 19 th. Century, *Indian Economic and Social History Review (I.E.S.H.R.),* Delhi, Vol. 1, No. 1. July-Sep. 1963.

Morris, David Moris. "Economic Change and Agriculture in Nineteenth Century India", *I.E.S.H.R,* Delhi, Vol. III, No.2, June, 1966.

Nayeem, M.A. " Mughal Documents Relating to the Peishscush of the Zamindars of South India", *I.E.S.H.R,* Delhi, Vol. XII, No. 4, Oct-Dec. 1975.

Reddy,D. Krishna. Naati Viprapuri, Neti Uppanelli" Tel. *Andhra Prabha*, Bangalore, 4 March, 1978.

Reddy, D. Narasimha. "Problems and Perspectives of Development of Irrigation in D.P.A.: A case Study of Anantapur District," in N.B.K. Reddy(ed) *Proceedings of All India Symposium on Drought Prone Areas of India*, Tirupati, 1979.

Sarkar, Jagdish Narayan. " A Survey of Economic Conditions in India during the first half of the Eighteenth Century, " *Itihas*, Hyderabad, Vol.1, No.1, Jan-July, 1973.

Seshan, K.S.S. "The Great Famine in Punganur Zamindari, 1876-78", *Itihas*, A.P. State archives, Hyderabad.

Appendices

Appendix - 1

Hyder Ali's Parwana to Mummadi Chikka Royalu

(Hyder Ali's personal Seal)

After mutual compliments:

Sugutur Immadi Chikka Royalu, the Palegar of Punganur had come to the Huzur and while engaged in the war, had passed away. It is now ordered his son, Raja Shankar Royal should succeed to the Punganur throne. Hence this order is sent from the Huzur through Dalwayi Papanna and Vakil Thammaji Pandith. Be it known that the said prince should be crowned with the usual customs and honours of the Samstanam and the matter should be reported back to the Huzur.

Dated, June 29, 1781.
Camp: Musallipaka (Wandiwash)

Appendix - 2

Lord Cornwallis Letter to Mummadi Chikka Royal (1791)

To:

Ruffurat Avali Nisha Mummadi Chikka Royal, Samsthanam Punganur, Bafiat Bashund,

I am in due receipt of the Arzi you sent me and I have the contents thereof. You have written that you have sent some articles through your Vakil Balaji Row to meet the requirements of army under Captain Read Sahib ; and that some more will be sent through the merchants of your place . Captain Read Sahib is in receipt of the above mentioned articles. Sheep have also been supplied to the army. The value of these items has been paid to your Vakil. By the services you have rendered, we have come to understand the nobility of your character and the prosperity of your country. You must improve your Samsthanam, and behave towards us trustworthily. You must also attend to Circar business carefully.

What more I have to say.

Dated: 17 December, 1791.

(Sd) CORNWALLIS

Appendix - 3

Tipu Sultan's Letter to Mummadi Chikka Royal

To

Raja Samsthanam, Punganur.

Whereas we are in receipt of the Arzi sent through your Vakil Thammaji Pandith, and we have come to understand, through your Vakil your welfare, and increase of your prosperity, and the confidence reposed by you in us, we protect you, and send you this Hukum, in consonance with your dignity, as per your request.

In addition to your paying to the Circar, the peishcush as per Kararnama, it is also ordered that the fort at Avulapalle should be levelled to the ground. After levelling the fort to the ground, an officer will be sent by the Circar to see if the order was carried out.

Two months after, you will be sent for, for a Royal audience. You should then go to the Huzur, pay us a visit, and after assuring an assurance of protection, return to your native land. If you only obey us with all your heart, every kind of protection will be extended to you. Rest assured, and act accordingly.

A *takid* has been issued to Sayyid Ali Amir to put you in possession of Ramasamudram and Chembakur.

Another Takid has been issued to Asandur of Gurramkondah, not to give trouble to the taluk Muzukur. A third has been sent to Meer Moohideen . Thus three Takids have been sent., and the orders contained therein will be executed.

You must continue to remit to the treasury.

Dated Jaffer, Fusli 1210.

(Sd) Khat Munshi Subba Rao

Appedix - 4

Kowlenama Given by Captain Graham, Collector of Barahmahal to Raje Chikka Royal of the Pungnoor Samsthanam

The whole villages of Punganoor Samsthanam have hitherto remained attached to the Company Government and the Mysore Circar. They have now been divided into three shares, of which two were given to Kristnaraj Vodiyar, Rajah of Mysore and the remaining one was taken by the Company's government, peishcush on the villages composing the one share taken by the government, was fixed for the current *Siddarthi*, and the said villages were made over to you. You are to take possession of the said villages and pay to the government for the current year Siddarthi, the amount of peishcush i.e. Beris, in Kantroyi Pagodas 6666 and 6 11/16 Fanams. The said amount should be paid into the treasury by the end of:

February:	Pagodas	2222
April	-do-	2222
June	-do-	2222 and 6.11/16 Fanams
	Total:	**6666 and 6.11/16 Fanams**

You must pay the sum in instalments in the treasury at Krishnagiri and obtain receipts. If eight days lapse after each instalment without payment, the sum should be paid with interest. Whatever balance remains unpaid would be collected together with its equivalent sum as fine. Moreover the one share of the villages taken by the government was thus given to you after fixing the Beriz as above. The other two shares of the villages were given to the Mysore Circar. In the event of your taking the said two shares you may do so after having the Beriz settled on them. If you get them on a decreased Beriz, you must pay the Company's government the same amount of Beriz settled by them as above (one share of the villages). If you get them, (the above two shares) on an increase of Beriz from the Mysore Circar you will have to pay the excess, in proportion thereto, on the one share allowed to you by government.

The miscellaneous Bhatavarthi Inams etc. should remain in enjoyment as usual. If thefts etc. occur in your jurisdiction you will be held responsible for the same. A statement showing the hamlets and Khasba villages taken by the Company's government for their share was given to you with a proclamation. You must get that proclamation explained throughout the Taluk and keep it with you. No repairs to the Avulapalle fort should be made without the sanction of government.

17 November, Fasli 1209

(Sd) Games George Graham
Collector.

Appendix - 5

Kowlenama of Diwan Purniah to Sankar Royal

I am quite well up to this date and expect your communication of welfare. In the year *Siddadree* two portions of your Samsthanam including Chadoomoo and Kandur were transferred to the management of Mysore Circar. But on the strong desire of Sobbarow Kristna Pradany in your favour regarding peishcush the fresh peishcush was fixed to the amount of 13,333 at odd Controy Pagodas as out of which he paid the sum of 5,683 and odd through the means of sowkars and for the standing balance to the amount of 7,650 Controy Pagodas he promised to liquidate it within the New Moon in the month of Anny of the said year and also executed a written document to Circar to that effect.

In consequence, I hope you both to discharge your balance within the time prescribed above.

I have the honour to send you two pairs shawls and that of Killuth for your acceptance and hope you both manage the Samsthanam with good order and prosper.

Chaitram, 1799. (Sd) Poorniah.

Appendix - 6

Revenue Despatch to Madras from the Secretary of State for India

No:14

Dated: 20 February, 1860

1. I have under my consideration in the Council the letter from your Excellency, dated 9th. November 1859, No. 64.
2. Her Majesty's Government have much satisfaction in being able to mark their sense of loyalty to the British government displayed by the Zamindar of Punganoor and his ancestors, combined as it has been, by a good administration of the Polliem held by them, and by the liberal and considerate treatment of the people entrusted to their charge and they are accordingly prepared so far as to comply with your recommendation in favour of the Zamindar, as to authorise you to grant him a lease of the estate on the conditions specified by the Board of Revenue in their letter of the 22nd December 1858, the terms to be subject to revision at the expiration of fifty years, and they accordingly authorise you to grant unto Rajah Sugatur Immadi Sankar Royalu Yashovanta Bahadoor and his heirs a permanent title to the Punganoor Estate, subject to the payment of an annual peishcush of 63 rupees in the form and on the conditions of the perpetual lease prepared by the Board of Revenue, and forwarded to you with their letter of the 22nd December, 1858.

(Sd) Sir Charles Wood.

Appendix - 7

Sanad –I- Milkedt Istimrar

(Granted to Punganur in 1861)

Sanad –I- Milkedt Ishtimrar or Deed of permanent property granted by the Hon'ble the Governor in Council of Fort Saint George, on behalf of Her Majesty's Secretary of State for India, to Raja Sugutur Immadi Shankar Royal Eshovanth Bahadur, Zamindar of Punganur, in the Zillah of North Arcot.

1. Whereas for a long series of years past, the estate of Punganur, lately attached to the District of Cuddapah and now included in the District of North Arcot, and consisting of the villages hereinafter mentioned, has been held on temporary leases by your ancestors and yourself and whereas your family has always been distinguished by its loyalty and good behaviour, the Hon'ble Governor in council on behalf of Her Majesty's Secretary of State for India, is pleased in consideration of the aforesaid circumstances, by this Sanad – Milkedt Istimrar, to grant the said Estate to you, your heirs successors and assignees in perpetuity, on the several conditions set forth in this Deed.
2. The assessment of your Zamindary is fixed from the commencement of Fasli 1270 at the annual sum of Rupees 63,000/ which is hereby accordingly, declared by this Sanad to be the permanent annual Jumma of your Zamindary, payable in the current coin of the province, in fixed instalments, agreeable to the separate Kistbandi signed by you.
3. This permanent assessment of the land tax on your Zamindary is exclusive of the revenue derived from the manufacture and sale of salt and saltpetre; exclusive of Sayer of duties of every description, whereby sea or land,

the entire administration of which the Government reserves to itself exclusive of the Abkari or tax on the sale of spirituous liquors, and intoxicating drugs exclusive of Excise, which is or may be levied on commodities or articles of consumption; exclusive of all taxes, personal and profession, as well as of those markets, fairs and bazaars; exclusive of Lekhiraj lands (lands exempt from the payment of public revenue) and all other alienated lands paying a small quit rent which rent is unchangeable by you, is included in the assets of your Zamindary, and exclusive of all lands and Rusooms heretofore appropriated to the support of Police establishments The Government reserves to itsel the entire exercise of its discrction in continuing or abolishing temporarily, or permanently the items of revenue included, according to the custom and practice of the country, under several heads above stated.

4. You shall regularly pay in all seasons the amount of Permanent assessment above fixed, the remissions which have occasionally been granted according to the custom of the country and never on account of draught, inundation or other calamity of the season, shall now cease and never be revived, and if (which God forbid) you should fail to discharge your engagements, your Zamindari and your persona property shall be answerable for the consequence of such a failure.

5. In this event, your property and your Estate will be liable to be attached and sold for the payment of the public revenue. But under the moderate terms of the assessment on your Zamindary, this event can never happen except in consequence of your own default, for the courts of judicature will protect you against such an injury unless warranted by your failure.

6. You shall be at free liberty, to transfer, without the previous consent of Government or of any other authority to whomsoever you may think proper, either by sale, gift or otherwise, your proprietary right in the whole or in any part of your Zamindari, such transfers of your land shall be valid, and recognised by the court and officers of Government, provided they shall not be repugnant to the Mohammadan or Hindu law, or to the Regulations of the British Government. But unless such sale, gift or transfer shall have been regularly registered at the office of the Collector, and unless the public assessment shall have been previously determined, and fixed on such separate portions of your Estate by the Collector, such sale, gift or transfer, shall be of no legal force or effect, nor such transaction exonerate you from the payment of any part of the public land tax assessed on your entire Zamindary previously such transfer, but the whole Zamindary shall continue to be answerable to the total land tax, in the same manner as if no such transaction had occurred.
7. In the event of any sale of any part of your Zamindary for the liquidation of arrears of assessment; or in satisfaction of the Decree of a court of judicature, or in the event of transfer of any part of your Zamindary by gift, sale or otherwise, you shall furnish the Collector with true and correct accounts of your entire Zamindary, and of one portion of your Zamindary to be so separated, for a period not less than three years preceding such sale or transfer in order that the due proportion of the public revenue may be fixed thereon. The assessment to be settled on the separated part of your lands shall always bear the same proportion to the actual produce of the separate portion as the total payment Jumma on your

Zamindary, bears to the actual produce of the whole Zamindary, so that, if the y you, and shall increase of the fixed Jumma be ever made, under whatever changes or improvements your interests or your pleasure may lead you to introduce in to your Zamindary.

8. Although you shall have free right and liberty to transfer by sle, gift or otherwise, any part of your Zamindary, not repugnant to the regulations of Government, yet it shall not be competent for you to form any part of your lands into a separate estate with a less annual Jumma than (500 Star Pagodas) or Rupees 1,750/, except in accordance with the Regulation I of 1819.

9. In order that you may at all times be able to comply with the conditions of the 7th. Article of this Sanad, by which you are bound to furnish true and correct accounts of your Zamindary when required by the Collector, you shall support the regular and established number of Currnams in the several villages of your Zamindary. The Currnams shall be appointed from time to time by you and shall obey all regular orders issued by your authority, but they shall not be liable to be removed from their offices, except by the sentence of a Court of judicature. In the even of your having or of your under-farmers, tenants or ryots, having cause of complaint against Currnam of any village, for a breach of duty, you shall be at liberty to institute, at your own peril, a suite in the Adalaut of the Zillah, for the purpose of bringing such Currnams to trial and punishment, but in the event of your dispossessing a Currnam of his office without such regular process, you shall be liable to make such satisfaction for the injury was the Adalaut of the Zillah may decree. When a Currnam may be dismissed from his office by the sentence of a court of judicature, you

shall in the first instance select a successor from the family of the last incumbent, provided any member of that family shall be capable of the duty of the Currnam but if no member of it shall be capable of discharging that debt, you shall exercise your discretion in the appointment of a proper person. The name of the person appointed to succeed shall be reported to the Collector.

10. The Government having charged itself with the maintenance of the police of the country, will defray the entire expense of that establishment, you shall nevertheless aid assist its officers in apprehending and securing offenders of all description and you shall enquire and give notice to the proper authorities, of all robbers of disturbers of the public peace who may be found or who may seek refuge in your Zamindary.

11. You shall enter into engagements with your ryots either for a rent in money or in kind and shall grant to each ryot a patta or cowle, clearly defining the amount to be paid by him and explaining every condition of the engagement, and you shall grant or cause to be granted regular receipts to the ryots for all discharges in money or in kind, made by them to you, or for your account. If you shall neglect or refuse to comply with the demand of your under-farmers, or ryots for the pattas and receipts above mentioned, you shall be liable to be prosecuted under the Regulations and you shall also be liable to such damage may be decreed against you.

12. And whereas a survey and field assessment has been made or the lands of the Punganur taluk, and this assessment has been the basis of of the annual settlements during the last fifty years and more, and improvements have been made by ryots on their lands in faith of permanence of that assessment, it is hereby made a condition of this

Sanad that you shall in every case be guided by the survey assessment and by the establishment rules of settlements and shall allow, to the ryots the full benefit of improvement made by them in their land, and you will be answerable under Regulation IV of 1822 and the other Regulations and Acts applicable to the case, for any breach of this condition.

13. the foregoing conditions contain an abstract of the obligations and duties which you incur and of the rights which you acquire under this Sanad. The laws affecting your property will be administered by independent judges in constituted courts of judicature, governing their decisions by the legislative Regulations and Acts now in force or hereafter enacted which have been or shall be printed, published and translated for the information, and scrutiny of its subjects and on the Institutes of the Hindu or Mohammadan Laws, which are also open to the enquiry of all persons, the proceedings of the Adaulat will be held in open Courts accessible to persons of every description all parties will be a liberty to attend to their own interest by their presence in the courts during such proceedings, or to employ their Vakeels with such instructions regarding the mode of prosecution or defence, as may appear to be most eligible to themselves. The sentences of the court will be pronounced in the same public manner and executed by civil authority, without the imposition of military force; the Collectors and other public servants of the Government will be compelled to appeal to the court of judicature for the adjudication of all cases, in which by the virtue of their offices they may be parties; and finally the greatest practicable degree of scrutiny has been extended to the native subjects of the British

Government by the establishment of a gradation of appeals from Court to Court.

14. Being therefore sensible of the benefits conferred on you by this Sanad, and confident of enjoinment of the fruits of your industry, you shall be punctual in your engagements with the Government, you shall conduct yourself with good faith towards your ryots, whose prosperity is inseparably connected with your own; you should treat them with tenderness encourage them to improve, and extend the cultivation of the land, and thus lay the foundation of your own happiness in the permanent property of your Zamindary.
15. Continuing to perform the above stipulations and to perform the duties of allegiance to the British Government, its laws and Regulations, you are hereby authorised and empowered to hold in perpetuity to your heirs, successors and assigns, at the permanent assessment herein named, as Zamindary of Punganur. Given in Fort Saint George this first day of February, 1861 by and in the name of the Hon'ble the Governor in Council, Entered in Secretary's office.

By order of the Hon'ble the Governor in Council

(Sd)

SECRETARY TO GOVERNMENT

(Sd)

GOVERNOR OF MADRAS

Index

G

H

I

T